Acknowledgements

The authors would like to thank all those who willingly donated scores, photographs, background or specific information on the various subject matter contained in this publication. The task of collating all of the contents was difficult, but would have been impossible without assistance. Many thanks.

Copyright 1999 by W Young and A Chatto.
All rights reserved.
No part of this publication may be reproduced in any form or by any means without the prior written permission of the publishers.

Foreword

Brigadier Melville S. Jameson CBE
Chief Executive and Producer
Edinburgh Military Tattoo

In embarking upon the creation of this book, the Authors set themselves a most daunting task. The degree of research necessary to unearth not only the original manuscripts but also the biographies of their composers was in itself a mammoth undertaking, added to which were the problems of collation and analyses of the material, to ensure it's presentation in a uniform and highly intelligible manner.

My own involvement with The Edinburgh Military Tattoo has only served to enhance my appreciation of the formidable skills shown by drummers of today and of the considerable impact they have had on the overall quality of band performances.

This publication will doubtless serve as a monument to those drummers of bygone years who not only evolved and developed the basic techniques in use today, but who also had the ability and foresight to leave written evidence of their rhythmic skills for our guidance and understanding.

I am confident that it will act as an inspiration and challenge to both today's drummers and to those of the next hundred years of Pipe Band Drumming.

Melville Jameson

Edinburgh, Scotland

1999

ONE HUNDRED YEARS
OF
PIPE BAND DRUMMING

BY

DRUM MAJORS

WILSON YOUNG   &   ALLAN CHATTO
(SCOTLAND)   (AUSTRALIA)

Drum Major Wilson Young

For some twenty-eight years, from 1947 to 1975, Wilson Young's career as a pipe band snare-drummer spanned from his native Carluke, Scotland, to ultimately the  internationally known Shotts & Dykehead Caledonia Pipe Band and The Red Hackle Pipes & Drums -- in the former as a corps member under the famous Alex Duthart, and in the latter as Leading Drummer.
During that time, he shared in the thrills of winning every Major Championship -- not once but on numerous occasions -- including in Band terms 'The Worlds' four times, and 'Champion-of-Champions' six times, and as a Drum Corps 'The Worlds', again no less than six times. In addition to the UK, his drumming has taken him to 17 other countries --- some of them on numerous occasions.

In parallel, as a soloist, Wilson's many successes have included one First and two Seconds in 'The Worlds Solos', and he established a reputation as a major innovator in the early 1970's with his incorporation of then unique bass and tenor scores in The Red Hackle's highly regarded multi- instrumental recordings of that era.

His deep commitment to the workings of The Royal Scottish Pipe Band Association stems from 1972 when he was invited into membership of The College, and to date he continues his interest in educational matters having been invited to join it's Music Board. As Curriculum Development Officer of that body, he was Co-ordinator of the group which authored the 'Structured-Learning Series' - - The Complete Guide to Piping and Drumming Certification.

Since 1975, he has been an RSPBA Drumming and latterly Ensemble Adjudicator, and for a period of ten years, as Vice Chairman of the Panel of Adjudicators, has played a central role during a time of great change to procedures and rules-of-competition. His ongoing membership of the Adjudicators Training Group and of the Music Board's Examination Group continues that leading role.

Wilson's interests in percussion matters have never been confined to Pipe Band Drumming alone. Over the years, his expertise has extended from dance bands through Brass and Military Bands to annual appearances at orchestral / operatic performances in the roles of timpani and percussion, and he can claim the probably unique distinction of having performed in London's famous Albert Hall, in both a Pipe Band and a Brass Band! From a famous hall to a 'Hall of Fame. In 1995, the 'The International Pipe Band Drummer' magazine published in the USA, balloted its worldwide readership to establish a Top-Ten -- whether past or present -- in the world of pipe band drumming. The winners were elected to be inaugural members of the IPBD's Hall of Fame. Naturally, and as to be expected, all ten winners of such an honour are featured in the pages of this volume -- and one of these 10 drummers, is **Wilson Young!**

Drum Major Allan Chatto

Born in Sydney, Australia in 1932 Allan Chatto's drumming career commenced in 1948 with a local Grade 2 band, and, keen to expand his knowledge, he also embarked on a correspondence with Jack Seton of the then Glasgow Police P/B.

By 1952 he had moved to New Zealand to join the then NZ Champions, Invercargill P/B, under Leading Drummer Jim Kirkpatrick (ex Ballycoan, Northern Ireland), from whom he took over in 1954.

The spring of 1956 saw him in Scotland to join the Grade 1 Glasgow Corporation Transport band with which he competed throughout that year. Following a winter at the SPBA College he then accepted an invite from another Scottish Grade 1 corps --- Rutherglen P/B --- under L/D Willie Corr, where he remained until his marriage and return to Australia in late 1959

There, he joined what was to become in the 1960's the highly successful Sydney Thistle Highland Police P/B, winning both National and State Championships. In parallel, Allan mirrored these achievements on the Solo Circuit by carrying off the Australian and State Championships, as well as undertaking numerous administrative roles in New South Wales PBA including motivating the formation of it's College of Drumming

In 1976 he accepted the full-time appointment of Leading Drummer with the New South Wales Police Pipe Band. The position was both as band L/D and as Tutor of the drum-corps. Thereafter he enjoyed numerous successes until the new State Government disbanded the band in 1989.

His continuing administrative duties saw his appointment as NSWPBA's Vice-Principal --- and later the Australian Pipe Band College (AFPBA), as Principal of Drumming, serving for 26 years in that position.

Since his retirement, Allan has continued a life-long drumming correspondence, exchanging information and drum-scores with fellow enthusiasts around the world. He is the author of a number of drum tutors and has lectured both in Europe and around the Pacific. As an RSPBA Drumming Adjudicator since 1986, he has also travelled extensively.

His wider interest in percussion led in 1990 to being asked to set up a drumming course at the Escola de Gaitas de Ourense, in Galicia, Spain. This led to his appointment in 1995 as an Adjudicator of Percussion by the Gallician Pipe Band Association.

INTRODUCTION

This publication sets out to collate – for the first time – all representative, or examples of Pipe Band scores from each of the 10 year periods / cycles of this century. In each case the 2/4 March has been used to best represent the standard of achievement prevailing at any given point in time.

Some Readers may find it odd to find tunes like 'The Highland Wedding', 'Lord Alexander Kennedy' and 'The Balmoral Highlanders', illustrated time and again throughout this Collection. It cannot be disputed however that drummers have consistently found these particular melodies very attractive in their suitability upon which to provide the greatest scope for rhythmic, syncopated innovation and to portray via his 'Settings', the drummers own interpretation of good pipe band accompaniment – as he sees it.

BACKGROUND

We know that within the British army in the mid 1800's, Pipe Bands were introduced into the Highland Regiments and towards the end of that century, civilian bands began to be formed.

In Scotland, solo piping competitions at local Highland Gatherings or Games were already well established and very soon Pipe Band competitions also began to take place.

All the skills of the modern pipe band drummer have evolved from around that period and the current high standards of playing technique and of the actual construction of compositions or scores is the direct product of the many fine drummers of yesteryear.

Sadly, relatively few of the scores written by these early composers and developers are still in existence. There are many reasons for this present state of affairs.

- Although it is known that some form of snare drum notation was in use within the Military from at least around the 17th century, in the early days within pipe bands, drum rudiments and rhythmic patterns were taught by 'rote'(the system of repeating again and again until committed to memory)

- When the use of notation slowly became established in pipe band circles, with the rapid development of techniques and proliferation of ideas, initial scores were quickly superceded by more complex arrangements. The need to store and record the previous ideas would then have seemed to be in many cases, unnecessary.

- Very few actual pipe band drum manuals or books were ever produced and the ones that have been produced are by individuals mainly illustrating their own scores with perhaps an occasional example by another of their contemporaries from the same era.
- Probably the most likely reason for this dearth of old scores is simply a mixture of apathy or lack of appreciation during the inevitable 'clearout' in the aftermath of a funeral. To the layman (or woman), old, apparently worthless paper scribbles would simply have been discarded.

SELECTION CRITERIA

It would be nearly impossible to list or include names of every respected drummer from the past; therefore the following definition or standard was created for names which would be considered for inclusion within this Publication.

"Only Leading Drummers of 1st Grade Bands or Regular Prizewinners in the Worlds Solos, who are considered to have been influential in introducing and developing throughout the years, the techniques which have led to the high standards currently prevailing." Please accept apologies if due to an oversight, some worthy names have unfortunately been omitted.

FINGERING

The long established 'LRLL' practice in pipe band circles, of indicating the 'fingering' often set out by the composer when playing a particular score, is considered by many drummers to be completely unnecessary. There is no doubt however that in consideration of the complexity of many scores, an indication of the fingering can be very helpful, especially to the less experienced drummer.

This publication will make use of the currently widely used "Monolinear" principle, devised in the late 1920's and accredited to Dr Fritz Berger of Switzerland. This system shows notes placed above and below a single straight line, Right Hand for above the line, Left Hand below.

Many of the original composers featured in this publication who did **not** indicate fingering have sadly now passed away and the accuracy of the fingering actually shown cannot be authenticated. The Reader may be assured however that in practice, 'it will work'.

The Authors

CONTENTS

Influential Drummers
1900 - 1999

Name		Era	Band	Section	Page
Anon.		**1900-20**	Drumming in the Army	1	1
Seton	John	"	Glasgow City Police		
Catherwood	Jimmy	**1920-30**	Dalzell Highland	2	9
Faulds	Danny	"	Banknock & Haggs		
Hamilton	Alex(AD)	"	9th Bat. A&S		
Seton	John	"	Glasgow City Police		
Catherwood	Jimmy	**1930-40**	Dalzell Highland	3	15
Craig	Willie	"	Dalzell Highland		
Dalrymple	Jim		Dalzell Highland		
Darroch	Andy	"	East Belfast (NI)		
Davis	Charlie	"	Red Hackle		
Donovan	Paddy	"	Fintan Lalor (Eire)		
Faulds	Danny	"	Banknock & Haggs		
Hamilton	Alex(AD)	"	9th Bat. A&S		
McGregor	Alex	"	Edinburgh City Police		
Merrigan	Tommy	"	Fintan Lalor (Eire)		
Scott	Charlie	"	Glasgow City Police		
Taylor	Jimmy	"	Dalzell Highland		
Turrant	Dan	"	Maclean		
Barrie	Jim	**1940-50**	Newtongrange	4	23
Blackley	Jimmy	"	Edinburgh Specials		
Boag	Bill	"	Edinburgh		
Cairns	Jimmy	"	Clan MacRae Society		
Catherwood	Jimmy	"	Edinburgh City Police		
Corr	Willie	"	Caber Feidh		
Crawford	Geordie	"	Shotts & Dykehead		
Duthart	Alex	"	Dalzell Highland		
Ferguson	John	"	Edinburgh City Police		
Gilchrist	Teddy	"	Shotts & Dykehead		
Gray	Jimmy	"	Muirhead & Sons		
Jelly	Gordon	"	Dalzell Highland		
Keogh	Sean(Bisto)	"	Fintan Lalor (Eire)		
MacGregor	Alec	"	Renfrew		
McCormick	Alex	"	Glasgow City Police		
Paterson	Willie	"	Clan MacRae Society		
Pryde	Geordie	"	Edinburgh City Police		
Ross	Frank	"	Red Hackle		
Rowe	Adrian	"	Fintan Lalor (Eire)		
Seton	Jack	"	Glasgow City Police		
Weir	Tom	"	Clan Fraser		
Clacher	Adam	**1950-60**	Michael Colliery	5	39
Colville	Alex	"	Worcester Kilties (USA)		
Connell	Alex	"	Renfrew		
Docherty	Alex	"	Muirhead & Sons		
Duthart	Alex	"	Shotts & Dykehead		
Gray	Jimmy	"	Muirhead & Sons		
Helie	Alex	"	Renfrew		
Hetherington	Bob	"	Red Hackle		
Hunter	George	"	Red Hackle		
Hutton	Jim	"	Muirhead & Sons		
Kerr	Jock	"	Shotts & Dykehead		
Kirkwood	John	"	Shotts & Dykehead		
Marr	Jimmy	"	Lochore		
McCormick	Alex	"	Glasgow City Police		
Millar	David	"	Dundee		
Paterson	Willie	"	Rolls Royce		
Pryde	Geordie	"	Edinburgh City Police		
Rea	John	"	Armstrong Memorial (NI)		
Reynolds	Kit	"	Ballycoan (NI)		
Robb	Andy	"	Red Hackle		
Ross	Alex	"	Red Hackle		
Splitt	Davie	"	Lochore		
Stevenson	Billy	"	Dalzell Highland		

(Continued)

Name		Era		Section	Page
Armit	Dave	**1960-70**	Shotts & Dykehead	6	51
Barnham	Billy	"	Robert Armstrong Memorial (NI)		
Barr	Bert	"	Shotts & Dykehead		
Boyd	Bert	"	Ayr		
Chatto	Allan	"	Sydney Thistle (Aus.)		
Clark	Willie	"	Clan MacRae Society		
Connell	Alex	"	Glasgow City Police		
Docherty	Alex	"	Worcester Kilties (USA)		
Duthart	Alex	"	Shotts & Dykehead		
Gibson	Frank	"	Ballycoan (NI)		
Hosie	Andy	"	Renfrew		
Hutton	Jim	"	Muirhead & Sons		
Mackay	Tom	"	Muirhead & Sons		
Montgomery	Bob	"	Edinburgh City Police		
Noble	Joe	"	Renfrew		
Rea	Bobby	"	Ballycoan (NI)		
Reynolds	Kit	"	Ballycoan (NI)		
Stevenson	Billy	"	Shotts & Dykehead		
Turner	Robert	"	Muirhead & Sons		
Young	Wilson	"	Red Hackle		
Barr	Bert	**1970-80**	Shotts & Dykehead	7	61
Brown	Tom	"	Boghall & Bathgate		
Chatto	Allan	"	NSW Police (Aus.)		
Connell	Alex	"	Strathclyde Police		
Duthart	Alex	"	Shotts & Dykehead		
Hobbs	Wayne	"	City of Wellington (NZ)		
Hutton	Jim	"	Shotts & Dykehead		
Kilpatrick	Jim	"	Shotts & Dykehead		
King	James	"	Dysart & Dundonald		
Lawrie	Doug	"	Queensland Police (Aus.)		
Mac Innes	John	"	Pipers Whisky		
McErlean	Willie	"	Triumph St. (Can.)		
Montgomery	Bob	"	Edinburgh City Police		
Noble	Joe	"	British Caledonian Renfrew		
Rea	Bobby	"	Royal Ulster Constabulary		
Scullion	John	"	Shotts & Dykehead		
Turner	Robert	"	Muirhead & Sons		
Young	Wilson	"	Red Hackle		
Brown	Gordon	**1980-99**	Boghall & Bathgate	8	77
Brown	Tom	"	Boghall & Bathgate		
Collins	Jim	"	Glasgow Skye Association		
Cook	Arthur	"	Lothian & Borders Police		
Corkin	Gary	"	Royal Ulster Constabulary (NI)		
Craig	Allan	"	Glasgow Skye Association		
Craig	Gordon	"	Glasgow Skye Association		
Cranston	Neil	"	Boghall and Bathgate		
Dawson	Harvey	"	78th Fraser Highlanders (Can.)		
Duthart	Alex	"	British Caledonian Airways		
Gillespie	Harold	"	Victoria Police (Aus.)		
Houlden	Jackie	"	Babcock Renfrew		
Hunter	Michael	"	78th Fraser Highlanders (Can.)		
Kerr	Willie	"	Shotts & Dykehead		
Kilpatrick	Jim	"	Shotts & Dykehead		
King	Jim	"	Vale of Atholl		
Kirkwood	John(Jnr)	"	Strathclyde Police		
Maxwell	Reid	"	Simon Fraser Univ (Can.)		
Noble	Joe	"	The City of Glasgow		
Parkes	Gordon	"	F/M Montgomery (NI)		
Rea	Bobby	"	Ravara (NI)		
Scullion	Andy	"	Cullybackey (NI)		
Scullion	John	"	Scottish Power		
Turner	Paul	"	Dysart and Dundonald		
Walls	George	"	The City of Glasgow		
Ward	Eric	"	Strathclyde Police		
Wilson	Barry	"	Shotts & Dykehead		

Ancillary Information   9   99

A brief history of the Military Drum
World Pipe Band Champions
World Drum Corps Champions
World Solo Drum Champions
Index of names

Section 1

1900 -1920
Influential Drummers

		Band	Featured Score	Page
		Drumming in the Army	Standard Beatings	2
Seton	John	Glasgow City Police	The Inverness Gathering	6

DRUMMING IN THE ARMY

The drum has had a long history in the Army. It has often been termed an *"Instrument of War"*. The drum was played with sticks or beaters to play various patterns of beats. These could be used to relay signals to soldiers during warfare. Drums at this time were constructed much deeper than in modern times. Snares were later added to give the drum greater *"snap"* and carrying power.

Early Company **Drummers in the British Army** usually came under the command of the Colonel of the Regiment, but many Companies also had a drummer under their own command. Regimental drummers were taught the *"Beats or Signals"* by a soldier having the rank of *"Drum Major"*. On the field of battle from the 14th century, the drummer played a most important part within the battle. These signals had to be properly learned to convey the Commanding Officer's exact instructions to the troops, be it to advance the troop, or retreat etc. Of course every soldier had also to learn and recognise the signal pattern to be able to respond to the Commander's instruction. **Army Drummers** were held in high esteem and wore distinctive and more colourful uniforms than the troops. They were also usually paid a higher rate of pay. In these early days, instruction to the drummers was usually done by *"Rote"*. This was committing the pattern to memory, by listening to the Drum Major instructor playing it over repeatedly. By the 17th century it would appear that drummers were in some cases shown how to write their signals or patterns by some form of *"Musical Notation"*. An example of part of an early 17th century drum beating is shown below.

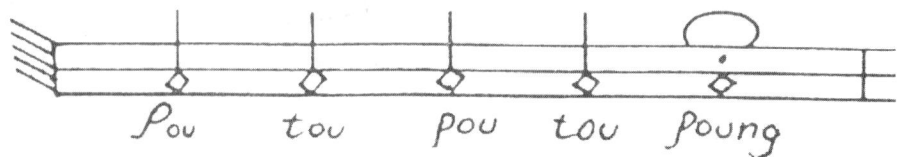

Two examples of early Military drums are shown below.

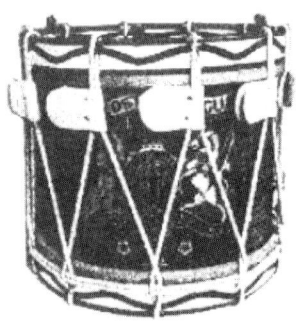

(a) Typical 16-17th century Long Drum. (Bass Drum)

(b) Typical 18-19th century Military Guards Pattern Side Drum.

Other musical instruments were gradually introduced into the Army. Firstly the Fife or Flute, and later the Bugle. All combined with the Snare Drummers and the Bass Drum to form the "**Military Drum and Fife Band, or Drum and Bugle Band**". When these and other instruments were introduced, the band became more ceremonial and was also used to lead the troops on the march. By now the drum was no longer used to relay Signals in warfare. The Regulation size (14" x 14") Side or Snare drum was introduced and the Bass Drum became much narrower.

In North America in the middle 1700's, Britain and France were at war and each had Drum and Fife Bands.

Part of a typical Military snare drum score from the middle of the 1800's is shown below.

From 1810 onwards, several drum tutor books were written. It is claimed that Dan Emmett wrote the first Drumming Tutor for the United States Army in the 1820's, and in 1861 he combined with George Bruce, to produce *"A Drummers and Fifers Guide"*, An example of a part of a snare drum score is shown below.

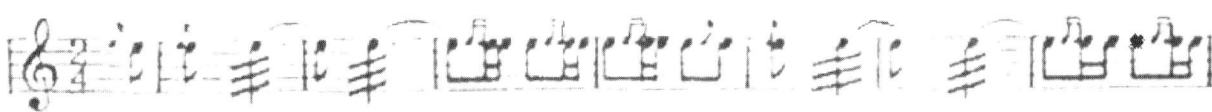

What style of drum score were the **British Army Drum and Fife Bands** playing during the early part of the 19th century? Henry Potter and Co, the famous Drum Makers of Aldershot, England, were established from 1812. They published a number of editions of their popular *"Drum, Fife and Bugle Manual"*. An example of a score for the *"Charge"* from the 1896 edition is shown below.

Below is shown the Drummers Position, from the 1886 edition of the Henry Potter, Drum, Fife and Bugle Manual.

The Great Highland Bagpipe was **officially** introduced into Scottish Highland Regiments within the British Army, in around 1854. Civilian pipe bands were soon to follow, and by the end of the 1800's, pipe bands had also been formed in a number of Police establishments in Scotland and elsewhere. Bands and band music became popular all over the world. It would seem reasonable to accept that initially the pipe band drummers would play similar beatings to those played by the Drum and Fife Band drummers. The **Fundamental Rudiments** of Snare Drumming are the same for any idiom. Later the pipe band drummer would gradually adapt his score to suit the rhythm of the bagpipe melodies.

It would seem likely that the *"Tenor Drum"* was introduced into a number of Military bands in about the mid 1800's, but did not seem to appear or be accepted into pipe bands until the early 1900's. The Tenor Drum players at that time were more concerned with the spectacle of *"Flourish"*, than with keeping time. The *"Time Keeping"* was always left entirely to the Bass Drummer. The **Rhythmic Accompaniment and the Dynamics** was solely the snare drummer's domain.

Drum Major John Seton (ex 8th Argyll's) is credited with producing the first Tutor for pipe band drummers in 1922. This showed the score within the traditional five line Staff.

One of the many scores shown in this book was a combined score for the Snare and the Bass Drum.

In 1928 **Dr Fritz Berger** had introduced into the Swiss Army, his *"Monolinear System of Notation"*. A Single line staff, with the Right Hand Tap shown above the line and the Left Hand Tap shown below.
The basis of this notation system was introduced into Scottish pipe bands during the mid 1930's by Drum Major Jimmy Catherwood, of the Dalzell Highland Pipe Band.
In effect, what was accepted was a compromise between the two systems – standard Staff Notation as used by **Seton** and others but written above and below a single line in **Berger** fashion. By 1948, the new system was gaining in popularity and is currently used almost universally, by Military and Civilian pipe band drummers.

Some of the differences in the notation systems used by D/M John Seton and by Dr Fritz Berger are shown below.

In the early 1930's, an effort was made to regulate the bagpipe settings and drum scores played by Regimental pipe bands within the Scottish Division of the British Army, particularly for **Military Massed Band** performances.

In 1934, the Army gave approval for the publication of Book 1, the *"Army Manual of Bagpipe Tunes and Drum Beatings"*. This collection was to be used to select the tunes and drum scores to be played for massed pipe band performances. In 1936 Book 2 was published.

Examples of portions of snare drum scores from the above publications are shown below.

Today, in Scotland as elsewhere, whilst there are still many **Regular Army and Territorial Pipe Bands,** assorted governmental cutbacks have greatly depleted their numbers, with the loss of centuries of tradition.

Those remaining however, have continued to improve in standard, with many actively involved in Civilian Pipe Band Associations and competitions. **Army Drummers** from both Pipe and Military Bands can be justly proud of their history and traditions – still displayed today in such events as the spectacular **Edinburgh Military Tattoo**, held at Edinburgh Castle, Scotland, in August of each year.

DRUM MAJOR JOHN SETON DCM
THE GOVAN POLICE PIPE BAND

The *"Drum"* is said to be the ***oldest*** instrument known to man. It was widely used in battle to signal the Officer's commands to the troops. It was also used to lead the troops to battle and on Parade.

The Fife and other instruments were later used together with the drum to become what is widely known as ***"Drum and Fife Band"***. The addition of other wind instruments led to the formation of ***"Military Bands"***.

When pipe bands were officially introduced into the Scottish Regiments within the British Army in the late 1850's, each Regiment had its own "Pipes and Drums". By the 1890's there were 22 pipe bands in the Scottish Regiments. The drummers would have naturally played ***Standard Snare Drum Beatings*** to accompany the pipe tunes, similar to those that were played in the old Fife and Drum corps, with the Bass drum just beating to keep time. Tenor drums do not appear to have been introduced until some time later. Civilian pipe bands were soon to follow.

John Seton, from Dunoon on the Argyll peninsula, became interested in pipe bands at an early age. In particular, drumming fascinated him, and coming from a musical family, he soon also began to study music notation and its application to drumming.

Being of good build, he was accepted into Glasgow Police and later transferred to Govan Police Pipe Band. There his dedication to the study of drumming led to him being encouraged to write a specific drum score for each pipe tune the band played, so improving the variety and quality of beatings.

Some years later, John Seton ('Pop' as he was affectionately known) was to write two tutor books for pipe band drummers, the first in 1922, and the second in the late 1950's. He is considered to be the first documented writer of Scottish Pipe Band drum scores, using accepted musical notation.

Below is a typical John Seton snare drum score for the tune, "The Inverness Gathering", circa 1919, from the "P/M Willie Gray – D/M John Seton Collection", published in Glasgow, 1922.

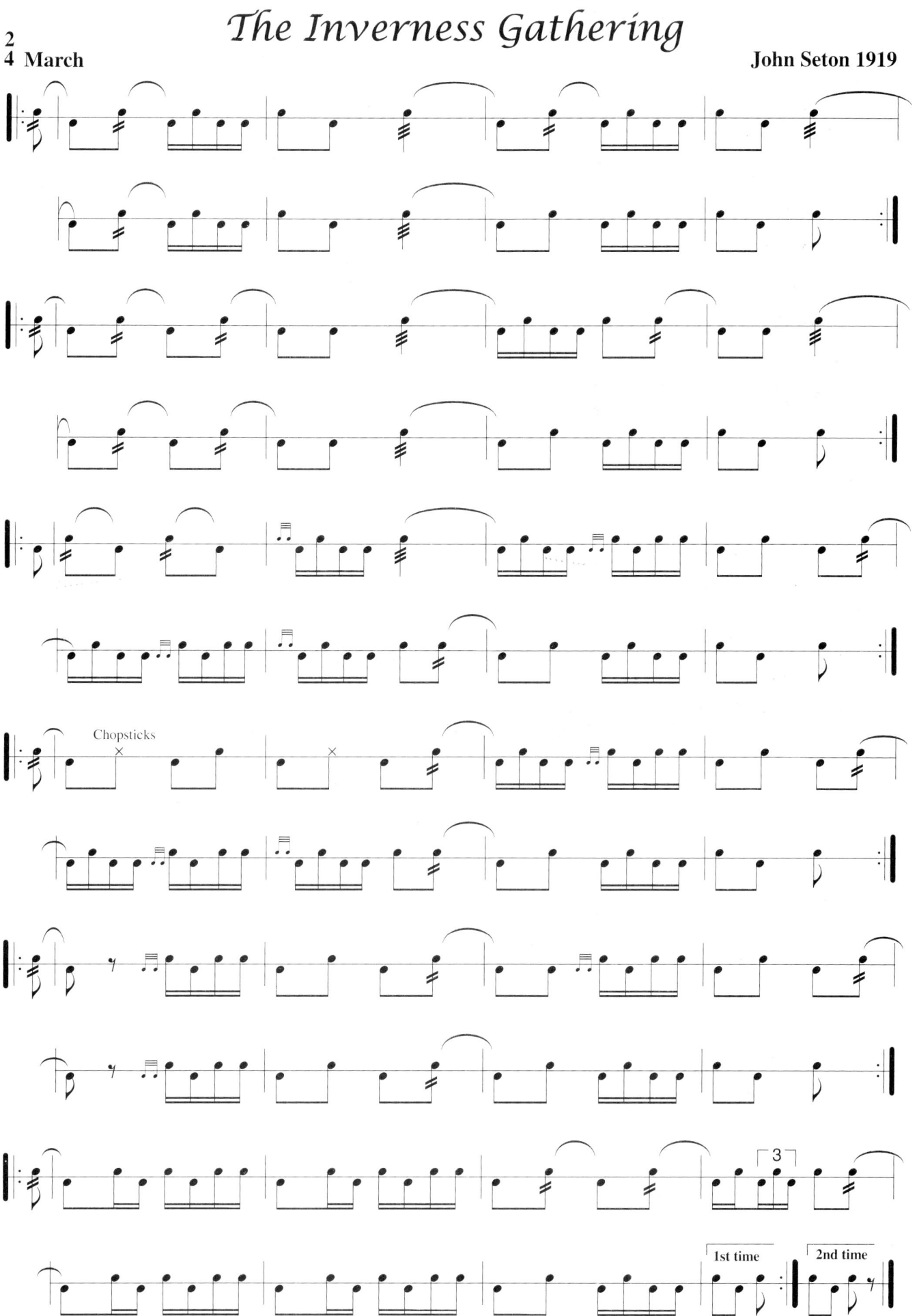

Section 2

1920 - 1930
Influential Drummers

		Band	Featured Score	Page
Catherwood	Jimmy	Dalzell Highland		
Faulds	Danny	Banknock & Haggs		
Hamilton	Alex (AD)	9th Bat.A & S	Colonel Stockwell	10
Seton	John	Glasgow City Police	The Balmoral Highlanders	12

DRUM MAJOR A. DOUGLAS (A.D.) HAMILTON, DCM
SEAFORTH HIGHLANDERS PIPE BAND
9th Batt. ARGYLL & SUTHERLAND HIGHLANDERS

Douglas "AD" Hamilton was one of the great pipe band drummers and Educators of the 1920's and 30's. He was D/M in The Seaforth Highlanders Pipe Band during the 1914-18 Great War. Upon returning to civilian life he studied music seriously and began to play in local orchestras and bands, and also tutored pipe bands in the Glasgow area. At the end of the 1920's he was appointed Drum Major of the 9th (Dumbartonshire) Batt. Argyll & Sutherland Highlanders. In addition, "AD" played percussion in the Glasgow City Orchestra on a full time basis.

In 1931 he published the well-received "DRUM SCORES", a collection of scores for Side Drum, Tenor & Bass Drum. "AD" was well respected and wrote a number of technical articles that were published in the "Piper & Dancer" magazine. In 1936 "AD" and D/M John Seton were asked by the Scottish Pipe Band Association to jointly assist in establishing a "Pipe Band College". For numerous reasons however it was not until after the 1939 - 45 War that one was fully established. He was later to be appointed Musical Director of the SPBA and also became involved in Drumming Adjudication. "AD" was a great advocate of the "Integrated Approach", where the pipe melody, together with the total drum accompaniment of Snare, Bass and Tenor drums, are considered as a single integrated unit, in an effort to enhance the overall band performance. Alex Hamilton was the prime mover for the introduction of "Ensemble", a concept that many were by this time supporting. He lectured strongly on the subject at many of the SPBA Seminars. A great number of bands in Scotland owe their drumming successes to Douglas "A.D." Hamilton, a fine knowledgeable musician, with a great personality. He sadly passed away in the 1970's. Following is a score from his 1931 publication.

AD Hamilton

Col. Stockwell.

DRUM MAJOR JOHN SETON DCM, BEM
CITY OF GLASGOW POLICE PIPE BAND

It could be said that D/M John (Pop) Seton, was the father of pipe band drumming, as it is known today. As a young man he joined the highly successful **Govan Police Pipe Band** shortly before its name was changed to *The City of Glasgow Police Pipe Band*.

During the 1914-18 war John served with distinction with the 93rd Highlanders. There, he extended his studies in music theory and notation to enable him to write out his drum scores, (a rarity in those early days).

In 1922, John Seton and P/M Willie Gray produced what is thought to be the first combined collection of pipe and drum scores. An injury to John's right hand in an accident involving explosives forced his retirement from active playing, but he continued to lead the band in the position of Drum Major.

In 1936 the SPBA College, at its initial formation, appointed John Seton and A.D.Hamilton, as joint Principals of Drumming. Later John was appointed Senior Drum Major to the SPBA and led the Massed Bands at all major championships in Scotland.

In 1950 John Seton and his family emigrated from Scotland to New Zealand. In 1954, he published another drum tutor, "50 Years Behind the Drum". This tutor included a number of scores composed by well-known pipe band drummers.

He continued with his pipe band interests in New Zealand but sadly passed away some years later.

The Balmoral Highlanders

2/4 March — John Seton 1927

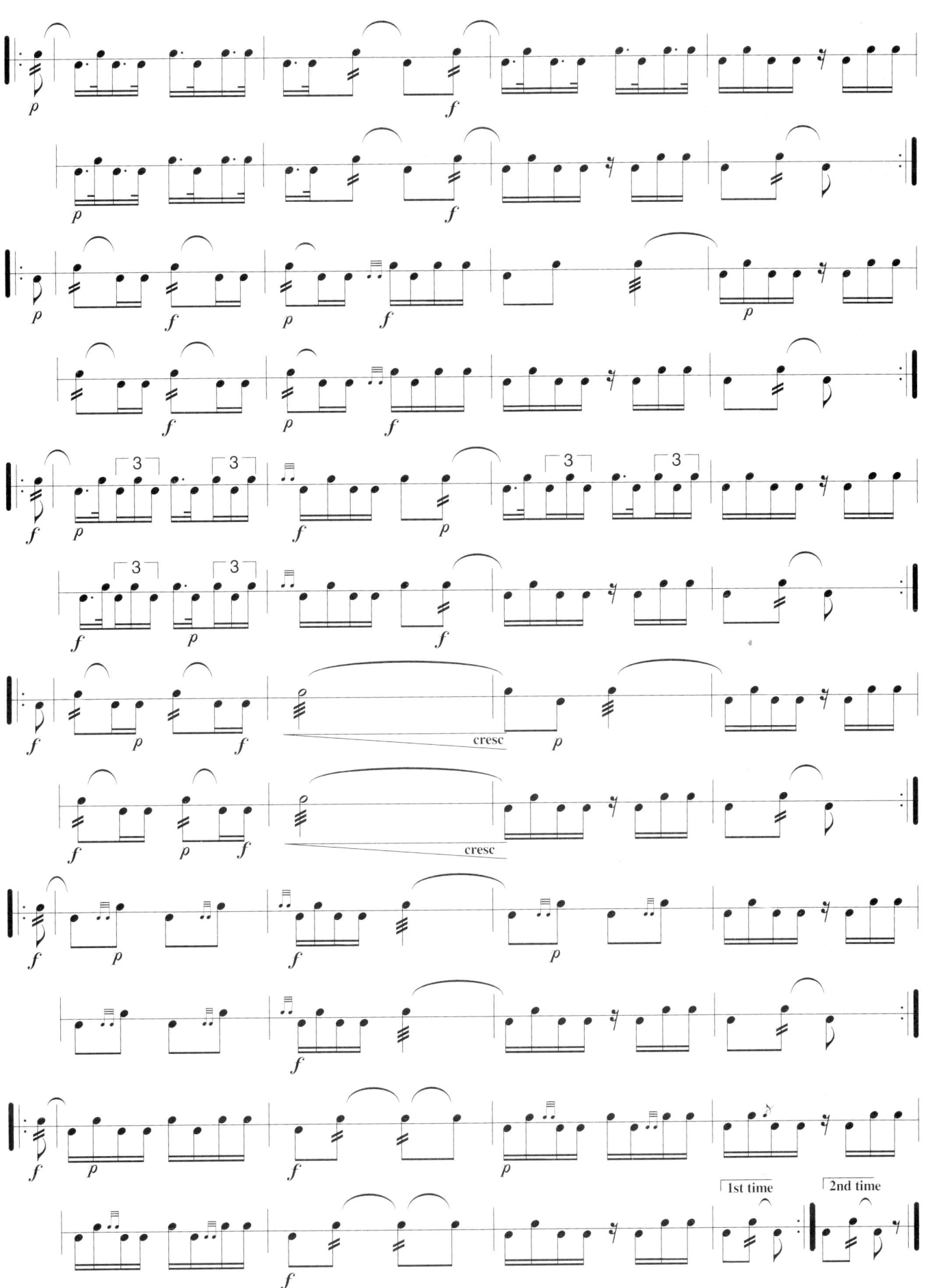

Section 3

1930 - 1940
Influential Drummers

		Band	Featured Score	Page
Catherwood	Jimmy	Dalzell Highland		
Craig	Willie	Dalzell Highland		
Dalrymple	Jim	Dalzell Highland		
Darroch	Andy	East Belfast (NI)		
Davis	Charlie	Red Hackle	The Orphan	16
Donovan	Paddy	Fintan Lalor (Eire)	The Highland Wedding	18
Faulds	Danny	Banknock & Haggs		
Hamilton	Alex(AD)	9th Bat. A&S		
McGregor	Alex	Edinburgh City Police		
Merrigan	Tommy	Fintan Lalor (Eire)		
Scott	Charlie	Glasgow City Police		
Taylor	Jimmy	Dalzell Highland		
Turrant	Dan	Maclean	"Highland Weddin"	20

DRUM MAJOR CHARLIE DAVIS
GLASGOW CORPORATION TRANSPORT PIPE BAND
THE RED HACKLE PIPES AND DRUMS

Very little is known as to how Charlie Davis started in pipe bands. However he was a very prominent drummer in Scotland during the late 1920's, the 1930's and 40's. He was obviously well

trained in musical notation as evidenced by several surviving well-written and rhythmic scores. In the mid 1930's he established himself as one of the leading drummers in the Glasgow area, his band the Glasgow Transport, won the Worlds at Cowal. Then in 1937, Charlie won the SPBA Individual Solo Drumming Championships.

As tutor to a number of the leading corps and players in the Glasgow area, his influence is regarded as considerable. After the war he played with the Red Hackle Pipe Band, and was later appointed by the SPBA as a Drumming Adjudicator officiating at many major pipe band contests in Scotland and also in Northern Ireland.

In 1953, due to ill health, Charlie emigrated from Scotland to South Africa where he was involved in tutoring a number of bands. During the City of Edinburgh Police Pipe Band visit to Southern Rhodesia in 1953 to take part in the Rhodes Centenary Exhibition, Charlie Davis together with Drum Major Geordie Pryde of the Edinburgh Police adjudicated a two-day pipe band competition at Bulawayo. Shortly after this, sadly Charlie Davis passed away. Following is an example of one of Charlie's scores that he played in winning the 1937 SPBA Individual Solo Drumming Championship.

Charlie Davis named this the "Orphan" as it was not set to any particular tune.

DRUM MAJOR PADDY DONOVAN
FINTAN LALOR PIPE BAND (DUBLIN)

Paddy Donovan was born in Dublin, Eire, in 1892. In 1907 he enlisted in the 2nd Battalion of the famous Connaught Rangers as a "Drummer Boy". However after 3 years service he was discharged. He then re-enlisted in the Royal Field Artillery, where he served till the end of the 1914-18 Great War. He began to study music and played in a number of Flute and Dance bands as well as having an association with The City Symphony Orchestra as a Percussionist. At this time Paddy took a great interest in pipe bands and felt that the drummers could do more "than just keep the beat"- a principal being well established in Scotland during the mid 1920's.

D/M John Seton had published a book of drum scores in 1922 and many other drummers were changing the direction of pipe band drumming. Drumming technique was changing too and scores were now written to fit more with each pipe tune. Wishing to be part of this radical development, Paddy joined the Fintan Lalor Pipe Band (Dublin) in April 1932 as Instructor and Leading Drummer, to great success. In 1934 the band went to the Cowal Games in Scotland to compete and caused a sensation when they came 2nd in the Worlds Drumming Championship. In 1937 they returned to Cowal and this time gained 1st place in the Drumming.

In 1939 "the Fints" won the Worlds again. Paddy had set a new standard in pipe band drumming that was to influence everyone for many years. He corresponded and exchanged ideas with many of the top drummers of the day in Scotland and elsewhere. Many of his scores have survived. After the 1939-45 War he joined St Laurence O'Toole Pipe Band in Dublin. Sadly in 1949 he passed away. Paddy was an inspiration to pipe band drummers. Two of his sons were also notable drummers.

THE HIGHLAND WEDDING
March — By P. Donovan, Dublin (Fintan Lalor Pipe Band)

The Highland Wedding

March — 2/4

P. Donovan 1939

DRUM MAJOR DAN TURRANT
THE MACLEAN PIPE BAND
BANKNOCK & HAGGS PIPE BAND

Little is known of the early days of Dan Turrant. However he had a very competent drum corps in the MacLean Pipe Band (Glasgow) during the late 1920's and early 30's when the band was very successful in competitions. Dan was a keen musician, and his surviving scores show a sound grounding in musical notation and drum score writing.

The MacLean Pipe Band was the main force behind the establishment of the Scottish Pipe Band Association in Glasgow in 1930. The band was also very successful at Cowal and in 1937 won the Worlds Championship. Below is a copy of Dan's score for the March "Highland Weddin" played that day.

Later during the 1930's, Dan took over as Leading Drummer of another leading Grade 1 band, the Banknock and Haggs Pipe Band. They too were very successful in competition. It is believed that in 1939 when the Second World War broke out, Dan enlisted and served in a Scottish Regiment. Sadly he was killed in action. Unfortunately no photograph of Dan Turrant has been located, but during his time in the pipe band movement, he set a very high standard of playing.

"Highland Weddin"

Dan Turrant 1937

Section 4

1940 - 1950
Influential Drummers

		Band	Featured Score	Page
Barrie	Jim	Newtongrange		
Blackley	Jimmy	Edinburgh Specials		
Boag	Bill	Edinburgh		
Cairns	Jimmy	Clan MacRae Society		
Catherwood	Jimmy	Edinburgh City Police	The Braes o' Strathblane	24
Corr	Willie	Caber Feidh		
Crawford	Geordie	Shotts & Dykehead		
Duthart	Alex	Dalzell Highland		
Ferguson	John	Edinburgh City Police		
Gilchrist	Teddy	Shotts & Dykehead		
Gray	Jimmy	Muirhead & Sons		
Jelly	Gordon	Dalzell Highland	Lord Alexander Kennedy	26
Keogh	Sean (Bisto)	Fintan Lalor(Eire)		
MacGregor	Alec	Renfrew	Donald Cameron	28
McCormick	Alex	Glasgow City Police	The Duke of Roxburghe's Farewell	30
Paterson	Willie	Clan MacRae Society	The Clan MacRae Society	32
Pryde	Geordie	Edinburgh City Police	The Braes o' Badenoch	34
Ross	Frank	Red Hackle		
Rowe	Adrian	Fintan Lalor(Eire)		
Seton	Jack	Glasgow City Police	The Balmoral Highlanders	36
Weir	Tom	Clan Fraser		

DRUM MAJOR JIMMY CATHERWOOD
DALZELL HIGHLAND PIPE BAND
EDINBURGH CITY POLICE PIPE BAND

Born in Motherwell, Scotland, in 1907. Many drummers are of the opinion that Jimmy Catherwood (known as "The One") was the greatest of the early innovators and tutors of pipe band drumming. He joined Dalzell Highland Pipe Band about 1918. In addition to his pipe band involvement, he took a serious interest in musical notation and all forms of percussion. During the 1920's he tutored many local bands and in 1931 became L/D of Dalzell Highland. In that year the Dalzell Drum Corps was the first to play the new Premier Rod-Tension drums, winning the Worlds Drumming Championship at Cowal.

Jimmy corresponded with many drummers. He was greatly influenced by Dr Fritz Berger, the noted Swiss drummer and went to Basle to further his studies. Jimmy can be credited with introducing the Swiss "Monolinear" system of notation into pipe band drumming and brought Dr Berger himself to Scotland in the early 1950's to demonstrate the Swiss technique.

Jimmy joined the Edinburgh City Police Pipe Band in 1941 and led the drum corps to many successes. He had many pupils in and around the city and exchanged his ideas with many other drummers at home and overseas. Jimmy also taught other forms of tuned percussion and made all types of drumsticks. Sadly he passed away on 8th November 1983 aged 76 years. A typical score is shown below.

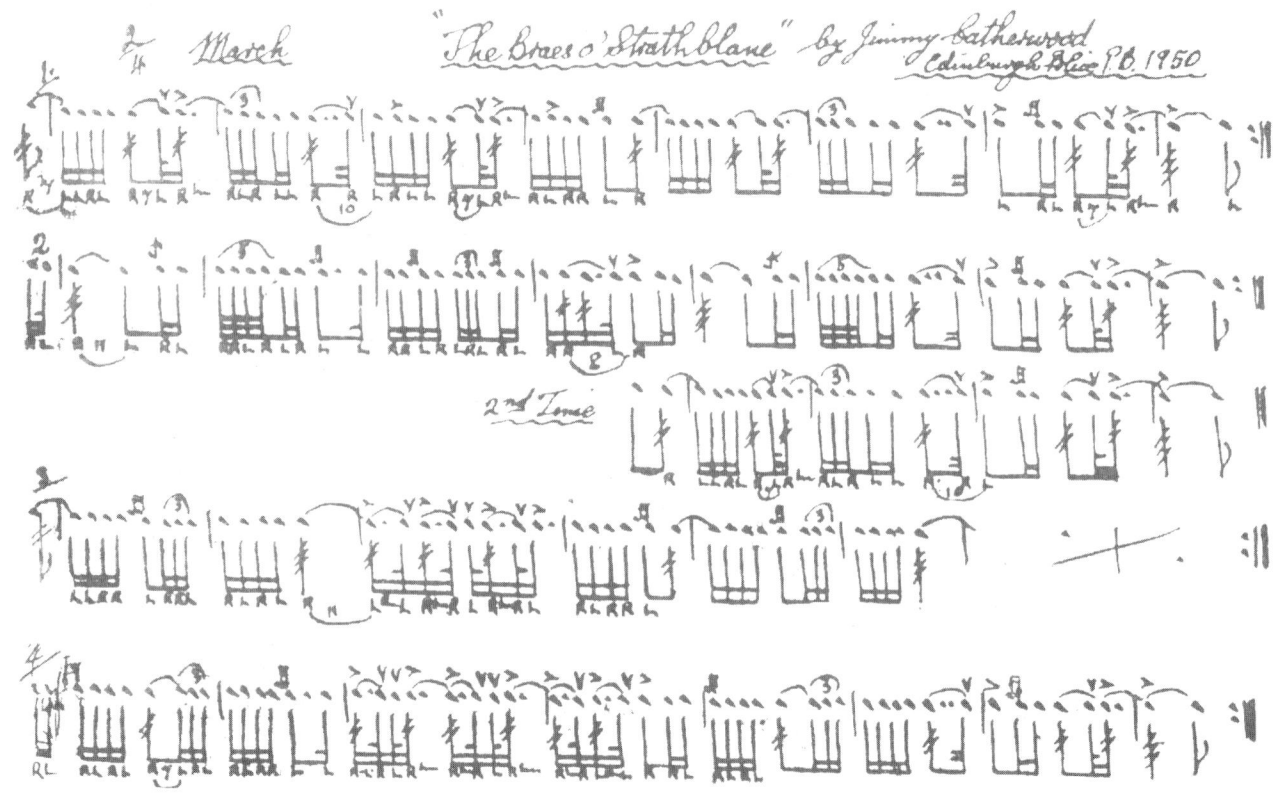

The Braes o' Strathblane

Jimmy Catherwood 1950

DRUM MAJOR GORDON JELLY
DALZELL HIGHLAND PIPE BAND
SHOTTS & DYKEHEAD CALEDONIA PIPE BAND

Born in 1915 in Motherwell, Gordon joined the local Boys Brigade pipe band at the age of 12, his Drum Tutor being Jimmy Catherwood, a player in Dalzell Highland band.

Gordon made good progress and at the age of 16 he was invited to join the Dalzell Pipe Band where Jimmy Catherwood was now the newly appointed L/D. The Drum Corps was successful in winning the Worlds Drumming Championships at Cowal playing their new Premier "rod-tensioned drums". The band and the drum corps were very successful in competitions over the next few years.

During the 1939-45 War, the Dalzell band was absorbed into the 6th Batt. Lanarkshire Home Guard and in 1941 Gordon became L/D. After the War the band reverted to "Dalzell Highland Pipe Band" and was again one of the most consistent and successful bands in competitions.

In 1949 Gordon left Dalzell to join Shotts and Dykehead. His expertise helped to win many prizes, both for the band and for the drum corps.
He later played with the Bucksburn (Aberdeen) band.
In 1952 Gordon and his family emigrated from Scotland to Australia where he was very much involved in the establishment of the Victoria Pipe Band Association College. He did not play in a band again but was kept busy as a tutor.

Gordon served for many years as a member of the VPBA College, as Tutor and as a Drumming Adjudicator. After a life devoted to the pipe band movement, he passed away in South Australia in 1996.

Lord Alexander Kennedy

2/4 March

Gordon Jelly 1946

DRUM MAJOR ALEC MacGREGOR
THE RENFREW PIPE BAND
NORTHERN SUBURBS SCOTTISH PIPE BAND (AUS.)

Alexander (Alec) MacGregor was born in Scotstoun, Glasgow on 20th October 1918. In 1930, Alex joined the 141st Company of the Boys Brigade and in 1932 he began learning to play the drum.

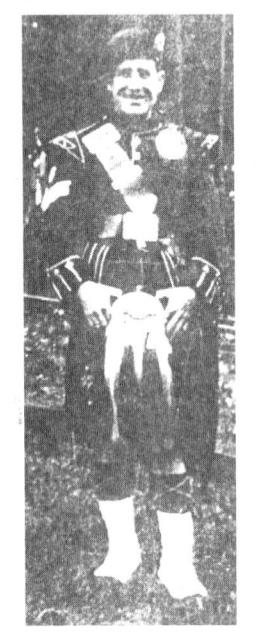

He joined the RNVR Brass Band in 1938, and then served with the Royal Navy seeing active service in the early part of World War 2. Released from the R.N, Alec resumed work at John Brown's Shipyards and in 1943, joined the Home Guard Pipe Band (Renfrew).

Alec's father was a piper, as was his uncle Gregor. Alec's brothers, Bill and Angus were drummers and by 1946 all three were members of the Renfrew Pipe Band Drum Corps. Alec was appointed L/D, and this Drum Corps, ably augmented at the 11th hour by Duncan Syme, was to win the 1948 Worlds Drumming Championship in Glasgow.

Bill emigrated from Scotland to Australia in 1948, soon to be followed by Alec. Then shortly afterwards, they were followed by the whole of the MacGregor family. There they joined the very successful Grade 1, Dulwich Hill Pipe Band.

In 1952, after settling into their adopted country, the MacGregor family formed the basis of the Northern Suburbs Scottish Society Pipe Band. Alec was appointed Leading Drummer and this band became a very successful Grade 1 combination. The band was to win many championships.

Alec, Bill and Angus were later appointed adjudicators in the NSWPBA Drumming Panel.

Sadly Alec passed away on the 29th April 1990.

Donald Cameron

March — Alec McGregor 1948

DRUM MAJOR ALEX McCORMICK
THE CITY OF GLASGOW POLICE PIPE BAND
THE CITY OF MELBOURNE HIGHLAND PIPE BAND (AUS.)

Alex McCormick was born in Clydebank, Glasgow in 1913. At the age of 21 he joined the local Flute band as a drummer. In 1927 Alex joined the Dalmuir Parish pipe band where the drum instructor was John Seton Snr. of the City of Glasgow Police pipe band. After a few years study, Alex had a good understanding of musical notation and playing experience. So it was in 1936 that he joined the famous *City of Glasgow Police Pipe Band*. His first parade was at the Cowal Games in that year, where the band won the World Championship, repeating this win in the two following years.

Alex was to form great friendships with other noted L/D's of the 1930's and helped to develop new ideas and techniques. In the late 40's Alex was appointed Drumming Principal of the SPBA College, Glasgow. Later he was to help establish a College branch in Northern Ireland. In 1951, Alex together with L/D Willie Paterson published a book of drum scores entitled, "The "Gaelic Collection". His Drum Corps was successful in winning the Worlds Championship in 1951 and 1952. Later that year Alex and his family decided to emigrate from Scotland to Melbourne, Australia.

In Victoria, Alex was responsible in setting up a Branch of the SPBA, holding examinations at all levels. He also played for some time as L/D of the City of Melbourne Pipe Band. Alex was very much involved in tutoring and adjudication in various States of Australia and within the AFPBA College he was the first Drumming Principal. Having spent a lifetime of involvement in the pipe band movement, Alex now lives at Sebastapol, Victoria.

The Duke of Roxburghe's Farewell

March

Alex McCormick 1950

DRUM MAJOR WILLIE PATERSON
THE RUTHERGLEN PIPE BAND
THE CLAN MACRAE SOCIETY PIPE BAND

Not a great deal is known about Willie's early days in the pipe band movement. Alex McCormick met up with him in Glasgow in the early 1940's and they remained friends for many years. A very knowledgeable musician and innovator, Willie tutored many drummers and successful drum corps, and both tutored and played with the famous Clan MacRae Society Pipe Band for a number of years. He was similarly involved with the Red Hackle and Rutherglen Pipe Bands and was a founder member in the 1950's of the Rolls Royce Pipe Band. He was a strong supporter of the SPBA College and a great advocate of drummers being able to read and write drum notation. Setting an example, he was amongst the first to successfully pass the College's Advanced Certificate.

Early in 1952, Willie combined with D/M Alex McCormick of the City of Glasgow Police Pipe Band, in the publication of "The Gaelic Collection". Its inclusion of many modern pipe band snare drum scores was well received and proved very popular throughout the pipe band world.

Willie retired from pipe bands in the early 1960's and went to live in England, where he passed away some years later.

The Clan MacRae Society

March
Willie Paterson 1948

DRUM MAJOR GEORDIE PRYDE
EDINBURGH CITY POLICE PIPE BAND
POWELL RIVER PIPE BAND (CAN.)

George Pryde was born in 1921 in "Nitten", (Newtongrange), a large coalmining village on the south side of Edinburgh. Later his family moved to "The Bogwood", a small hamlet nearby. At 13, he joined the Newtongrange Colliery Pipe Band playing with them for four years. His tutor was the famous Jimmy Catherwood.

With the outbreak of war in 1939, Geordie was called up for duty with the Royal Artillery. In 1940 he returned to the mines, rejoining Newtongrange. In 1941, Geordie joined the Edinburgh Specials Pipe Band serving for 8 years as L/D. The band was very successful in Grade 1 & 2 competitions. Geordie began to tutor other bands in the Edinburgh area. In 1947, he won the Worlds and also the East of Scotland Solo Drumming Championships. In early 1951, Geordie was invited to join the Edinburgh City Police Pipe Band. He remained Leading Drummer there until 1957. The band won the Grade 1 World Championship in 1950 and made the *Princes Street Parade* LP recording. The band also made a very successful trip to South Africa for the Rhodes Centenary Exhibition in Bulawayo.

Early 1957 saw Geordie and his family emigrate to BC Canada where he joined the Powell River Pipe Band. The band was successful in winning many major championships on the Pacific Coast.

It was a busy time for the band. In 1961 they released a successful LP recording. Geordie was appointed to the BC Adjudication Panel, and tutored at many Summer Schools in Canada and North America. He was also a very successful "Kit" or "Trap" drummer. Geordie Pryde has contributed greatly to drumming in both Scotland and North America. Retired, he now lives with his family in Powell River, BC Canada.

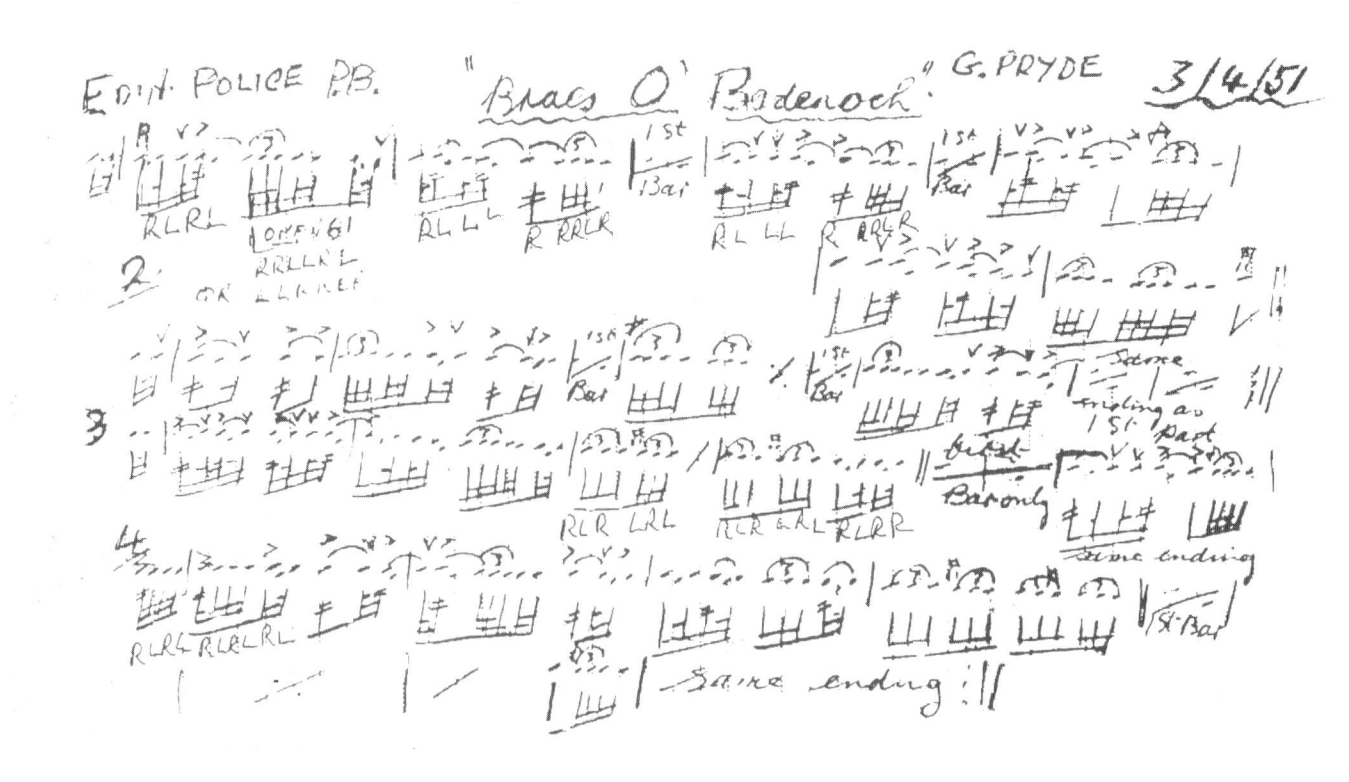

The Braes o' Badenoch

2/4 March *Geordie Pryde 1951*

DRUM MAJOR JACK SETON
THE CITY OF GLASGOW POLICE PIPE BAND

Drum Major Jack Seton was the son of D/M John (Pop) Seton, DCM MBE, of the City of Glasgow Police Pipe Band.

Jack took over as L/D of that band in the mid 1920's. He carried on the high standard of playing as established by his father and the band was a strong force in competitions. Jack was very interested in all forms of percussion and corresponded widely with other drumming enthusiasts. He was in constant touch during the 1930's with Bill Ludwig, a founder member of the USA, 'National Association of Rudimental Drummers'. Jack was eventually appointed an Examiner for that Association in the UK.

During the 1939-45 War, Jack was the Secretary of the Scottish Pipe Band Association in Glasgow. He also tutored many bands and individual drummers in the Glasgow area. Jack was also involved in other forms of percussion. His sister and brother Robert (who also played in the Glasgow Police) were both very competent snare drummers. The Glasgow Police Pipe Band was one of the most successful competition bands both before and after the 1939 – 1945 war.

In 1948, Jack and his wife, and son Ian, decided to emigrate from Scotland to Hastings, New Zealand. In his new homeland Jack was very active within the pipe band movement as a tutor and adjudicator, and published a regular drumming newsletter sent out to pipe bands by the local importers of the "Carlton Gaelic" pipe band drum. For a few years Jack played as L/D with the Hastings Scots Pipe Band, and also percussion in the Hastings Symphony Orchestra. After a long career, he sadly passed away some years later in N.Z.

"BALMORAL HIGHLANDERS" Jack Seton 1947

The Balmoral Highlanders

2/4 March
Jack Seton 1947

Section 5

1950 - 1960
Influential Drummers

		Band	Featured Score	Page
Clacher	Adam	Michael Colliery		
Colville	Alex	Worcester Kilties(USA)		
Connell	Alex	Renfrew		
Docherty	Alex	Muirhead & Sons		
Duthart	Alex	Shotts & Dykehead	Lord Alexander Kennedy	**40**
Gray	Jimmy	Muirhead & Sons	Dugald McColl	**42**
Helie	Alex	Renfrew		
Hetherington	Bob	Red Hackle		
Hunter	George	Red Hackle		
Hutton	Jim	Muirhead & Sons		
Kerr	Jock	Shotts & Dykehead	The Highland Wedding	**44**
Kirkwood	John	Shotts & Dykehead	The S.P.B.A. March	**46**
Marr	Jimmy	Lochore		
McCormick	Alex	Glagow City Police		
Millar	David	Dundee		
Paterson	Willie	Rolls Royce		
Pryde	Geordie	Edinburgh City Police		
Rea	John	Armstrong Memorial(NI)		
Reynolds	Kit	Ballycoan(NI)	Scotland the Brave	**48**
Robb	Andy	Red Hackle		
Ross	Alex	Red Hackle		
Splitt	Davie	Lochore		
Stevenson	Billy	Dalzell Highland		

DRUM MAJOR ALEX DUTHART
DALZELL HIGHLAND PIPE BAND
SHOTTS & DYKEHEAD CALEDONIA PIPE BAND

Alex was born in Cambusnethan, Lanarkshire on 7th October 1925. He started drumming under the guidance of his father John at the age of 8 and in 1937 joined the Craigneuk Parish Pipe Band.

Having gained some experience, he moved to Dalzell Highland Pipe Band whose L/D at the time was Jimmy Catherwood. In 1942, Dalzell amalgamated with the 6th Batt. Lanarkshire Home Guard. The Leading Drummer was Gordon Jelly, also a pupil of Jimmy Catherwood.

Alex progressed quickly; he had a natural sense of rhythm and music. The band was kept very busy during the war years and Alex entered a number of Solo drumming competitions, and was very successful. In 1949 Gordon Jelly left Dalzell to take over as the L/D of Shotts and Alex was appointed Leading Drummer of Dalzell. Many successes followed. In the next 5 years he won the Adult Solos 4 times and in 1953 the Dalzell drum corps, led by Alex, won the Worlds Championship.

Shortly after this, Alex directed his interests to playing the drum kit with various Dance Bands.

However in 1957, he was to return to pipe bands and take over the corps of Shotts & Dykehead Caledonia.

There, Alex established what was to become the new style of pipe band drum accompaniment.

His initial composition was for the march 'Lord Alexander Kennedy' and this really *"set the heather on fire"* in the Pipe Band world. Alex and his corps had many successes over the following years.

Lord Alexander Kennedy

2/4 March
Alex Duthart 1957

DRUM MAJOR JIMMY GRAY, BEM
WALLACESTONE PIPE BAND
MUIRHEAD & SONS PIPE BAND

Jimmy Gray was born on 17th May 1923, in the village of Brightons, near Wallacestone, Falkirk, Scotland. His father was President of the Wallacestone Pipe Band. When Jimmy was eight years old, his father decided that it was time for young Jimmy to take up learning an instrument. Jimmy decided that he wanted to be a drummer. He joined up with Wallacestone where he began to learn the basic rudiments. He progressed well and was soon playing in the drum corps.

When the War broke out, Jimmy volunteered for military service with the RAF. He served as a Wireless Operator, in many parts of North Africa.

After the war Jimmy continued with his drumming, studying practical and theory under the famous Jimmy Catherwood of Dalzell Highland. He then joined up as L/D with the very successful Grade1, Muirhead and Sons Pipe Band. Their successes continued over a number of years. Jimmy attained his SPBA College Elementary Drumming Certificate in May 1949 and his Advanced in October 1950. Later Jimmy was appointed to the SPBA College Board of Examiners as the representative for the Stirling Branch of the Scottish Pipe Band Association.

Retiring from active playing some years later, Jimmy developed a long association with the 153rd Highland Regiment, RCT (T.A). He served for 25 years as their drum tutor and Drum Major. Jimmy was honoured by HM the Queen with the award of the BEM for services to Army pipe bands. He also served as an RSPBA Drumming Adjudicator until his retirement in 1995.

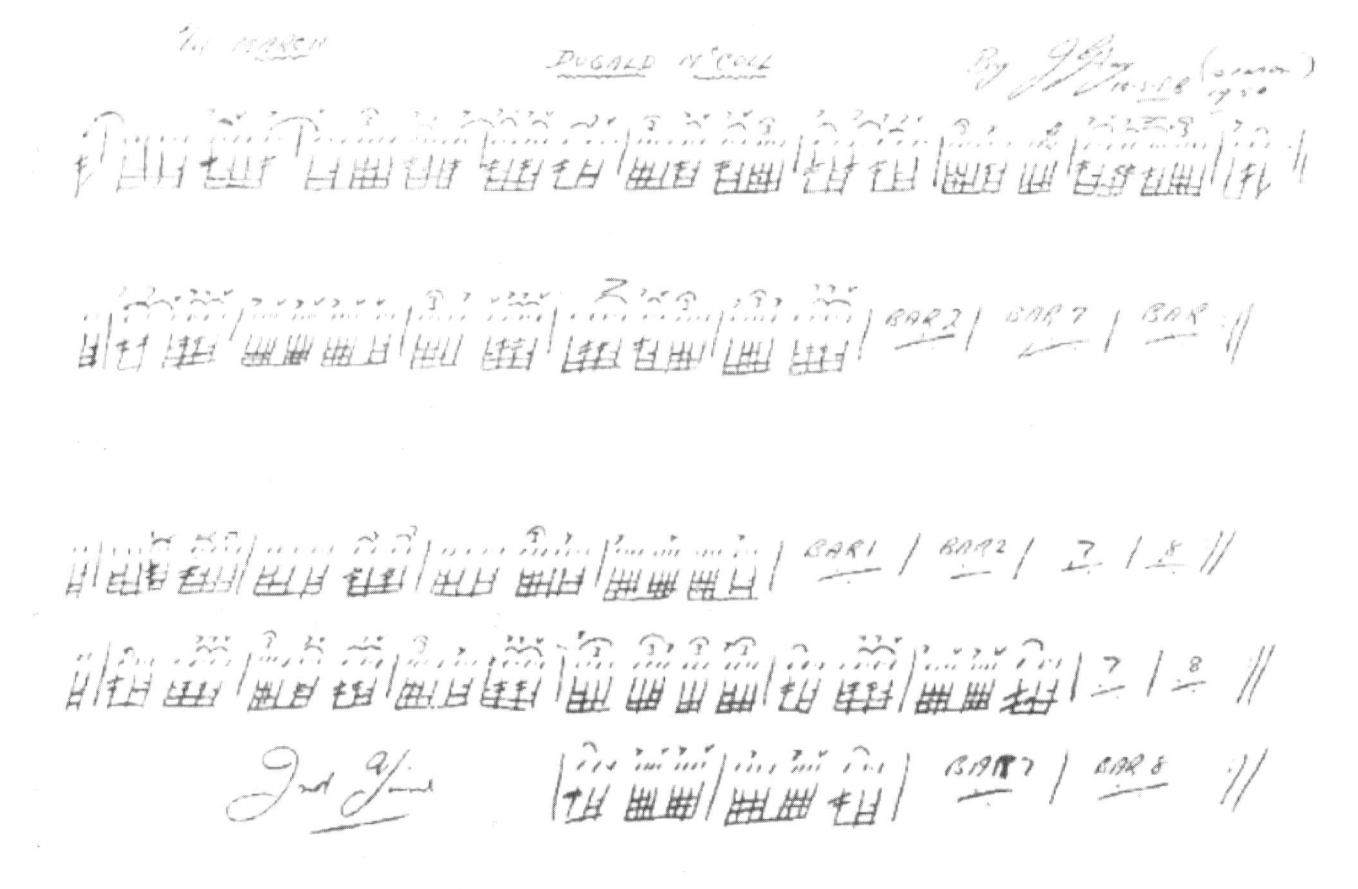

Dugald McColl

J.Gray 1950

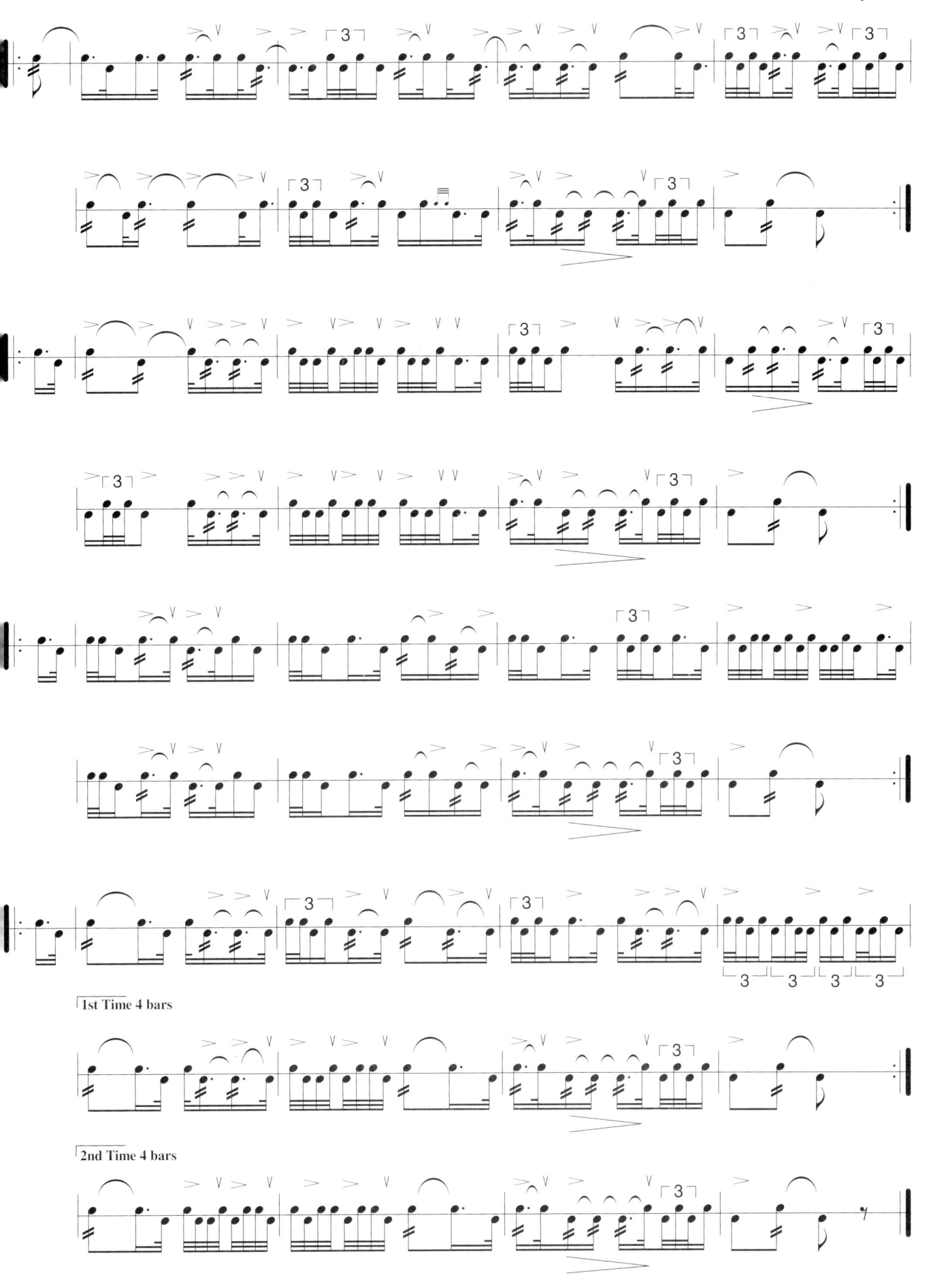

1st Time 4 bars

2nd Time 4 bars

DRUM MAJOR JOHN B. (JOCK) KERR
SHOTTS & DYKEHEAD CALEDONIA PIPE BAND
R.C.A.F. PIPE BAND (CAN.)

John Kerr was born in Forth, Lanarkshire, Scotland in 1929. He started pipe band drumming at the age of six, taught by his cousin Alex Colville, who was just a few years his senior. Within a year John was playing with the Kingshill Colliery Pipe Band. Here he received tuition from Gordon Jelly of the Dalzell Highland Pipe Band. Later he was to serve his National Service with the Royal Scots. When this term was concluded John joined the Shotts & Dykehead Caledonia Pipe Band and was Leading Drummer from 1953 to 1955. This was a memorable time for him as the band was a major prizewinner in competitions all over Scotland. In 1954 John won the SPBA World Open Solo Drumming Championship.

In 1955, John decided to emigrate from Scotland to Canada and joined the Royal Canadian Air Force. But it was not until 1959 that he joined the RCAF Rockcliff Pipe Band as L/D. The band was then under P/M A.R.Howie. They won many Grade 1 North American Championships and also visited Scotland. Eventually, after many years of military service, John B. Kerr was appointed the Chief Drumming Instructor of the RCAF. Discharged in 1981, he then joined the McNish Distillery Pipe Band under Pipe Major Gordon Tuck. 1984 saw him in Ottawa as L/D of the Dunvegan Pipe Band.

Jock Kerr was a major force in establishing a high standard of pipe band drumming in Eastern Canada. He has published several popular tutor books on drumming and he continues to be deeply involved within the pipe band movement. He now lives in St Catharines, Ontario, Canada.

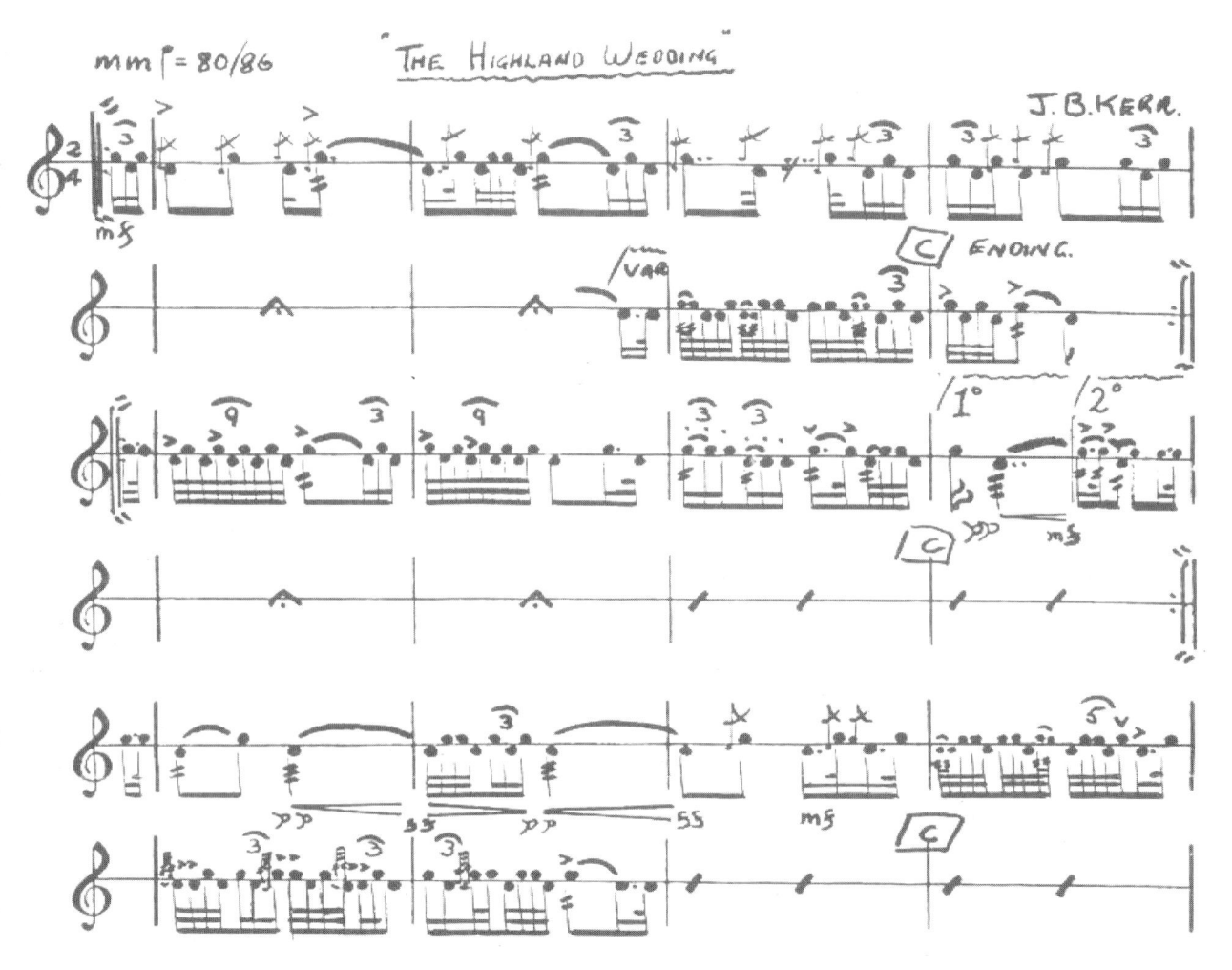

The Highland Wedding

JB (Jock) Kerr 1969

2/4 March ♩= 80/86

DRUM MAJOR JOHN KIRKWOOD
SHOTTS & DYKEHEAD CALEDONIA PIPE BAND
CLAN MACFARLANE PIPE BAND (CAN.)

John Kirkwood was born in 1928 in Newmains, Lanarkshire, Scotland. In 1939 when he was eleven years old John joined the local Newmains and District Pipe Band. Within a year he was playing with the band. As World War 2 had just started, competitions were few and far between and John had little chance to exercise his new found talent. The drumming played at the time was mostly based on the Army style, but things were changing. When he was 14, he met another drummer two years his senior, Alex Duthart. Neither was to know at this time, that they were destined to play a major part in the future changes to pipe band drumming. Each recognized in the other, a revolutionary spirit. John was to stay with Newmains for a further six years before he left to join up with Alex in the Dalzell Highland drum corps. There, they served under the famous L/D Gordon Jelly, a former pupil of the great Jimmy Catherwood.

In 1946 John was called up for Army National Service. While with the Highland Brigade Pipe Band in 1947, the band won the Grade 2 World Championship. Discharged in 1948, John returned again to Newmains, this time as L/D. In late 1949, he was asked to take over as L/D of the Shotts & Dykehead drum corps. He accepted, taking all of his Newmains corps with him. There they had many successes including the band winning the Worlds Championship in 1952. In May 1953, John decided to move to Canada and the whole of the Shotts drum corps also agreed to emigrate.

They all went to the St Catharines Pipe Band, Ontario. Later, the band decided to change its name to "The Clan MacFarlane". As well as being Leading Drummer, John was also for some time appointed as Pipe Major. The band had many local and Northern American successes. John always set a fine example as a great motivator, innovator and inspirer to his many pupils. Sadly he passed away in August 1972.

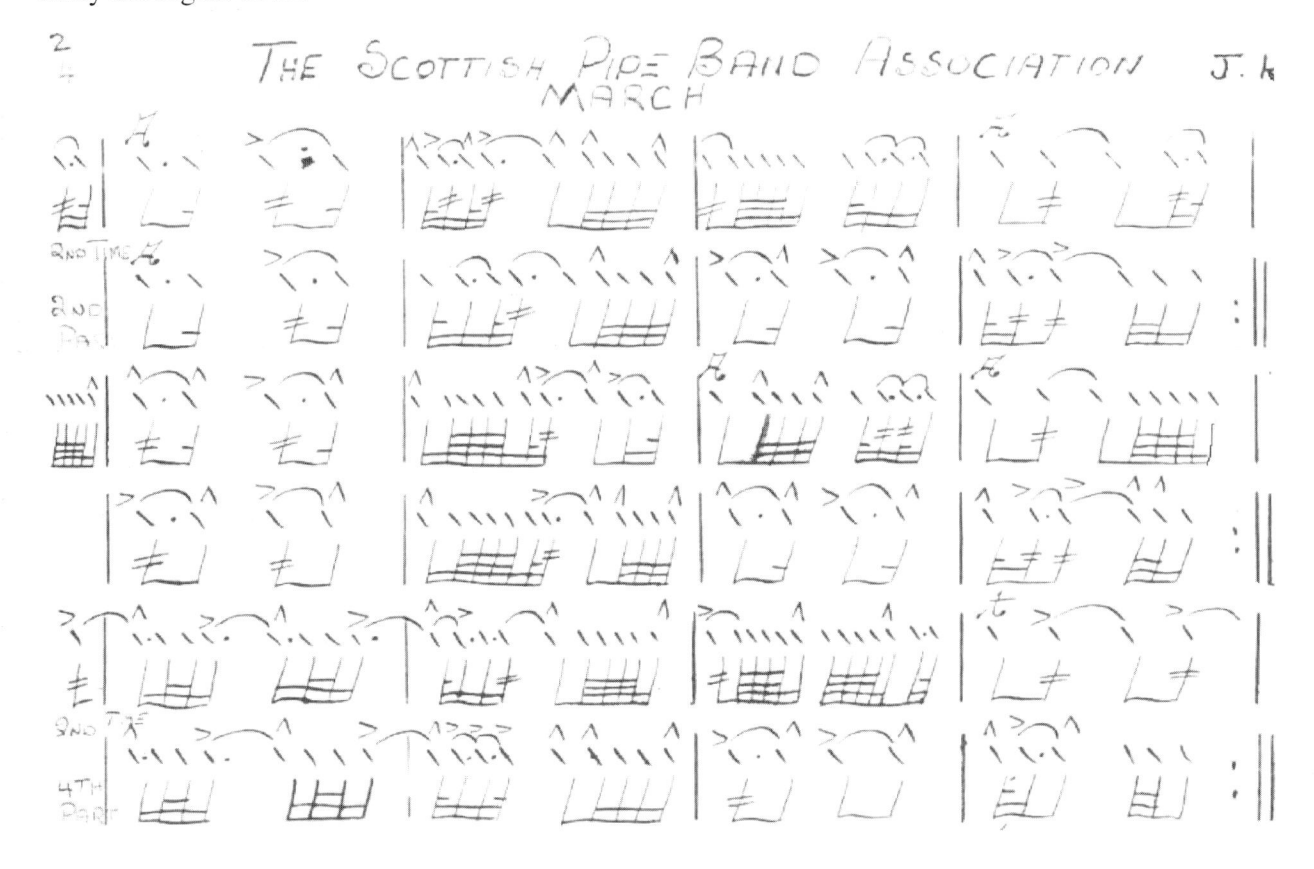

The March of The Scottish Pipe Band Association

2/4 March
John Kirkwood 1950

DRUM MAJOR WILLIAM "KIT" REYNOLDS
BALLYCOAN PIPE BAND
ROBERT ARMSTRONG MEMORIAL PIPE BAND
THE INVERGORDON DISTILLERS PIPE BAND

Born in Northern Ireland, Kit began to learn the snare drum with the Duke of York PB. He joined the Sydenham Pipe Band in 1943 and was made L/D in 1946. In the following year he left to join the Ballycoan Pipe Band as L/D, under P/M Billy Wood. A keen student of the theory of music, Kit sat all of the SPBA College Drumming Examinations and also the Elementary Piping, passing all successfully. At this time he was also in great demand as a Tutor and travelled extensively in Northern Ireland assisting pipe bands and drum corps.

After his spell in National Service 1953-55, Kit returned to the Ballycoan Pipe Band and led his corps to many victories until he left in 1962. He was then appointed to the SPBA Adjudicators Panel officiating at the 1963 Worlds Pipe Band Championships in Dumfries.

In 1964 Kit joined the Robert Armstrong Memorial Pipe Band and was appointed L/D. The band had many successes in NI and also in Scotland. In 1965, Kit was invited by Alex Duthart to join the corps of Invergordon Distillers PB. He accepted the position in the drum corps under Alex and enjoyed many successes with the band until it's closure in 1968.

A move to the West Coast of America saw Kit playing there for some years with a number of leading pipe bands. While in the USA, Kit was also a popular tutor and Adjudicator. He returned some time later to the UK. A most successful Leading Drummer, Kit was also a leading Solo drumming competitor with many wins to his credit, especially in the 'Ulster' and the 'All Ireland' championships. He continues as a member of the RSPBA Adjudicators' Panel.

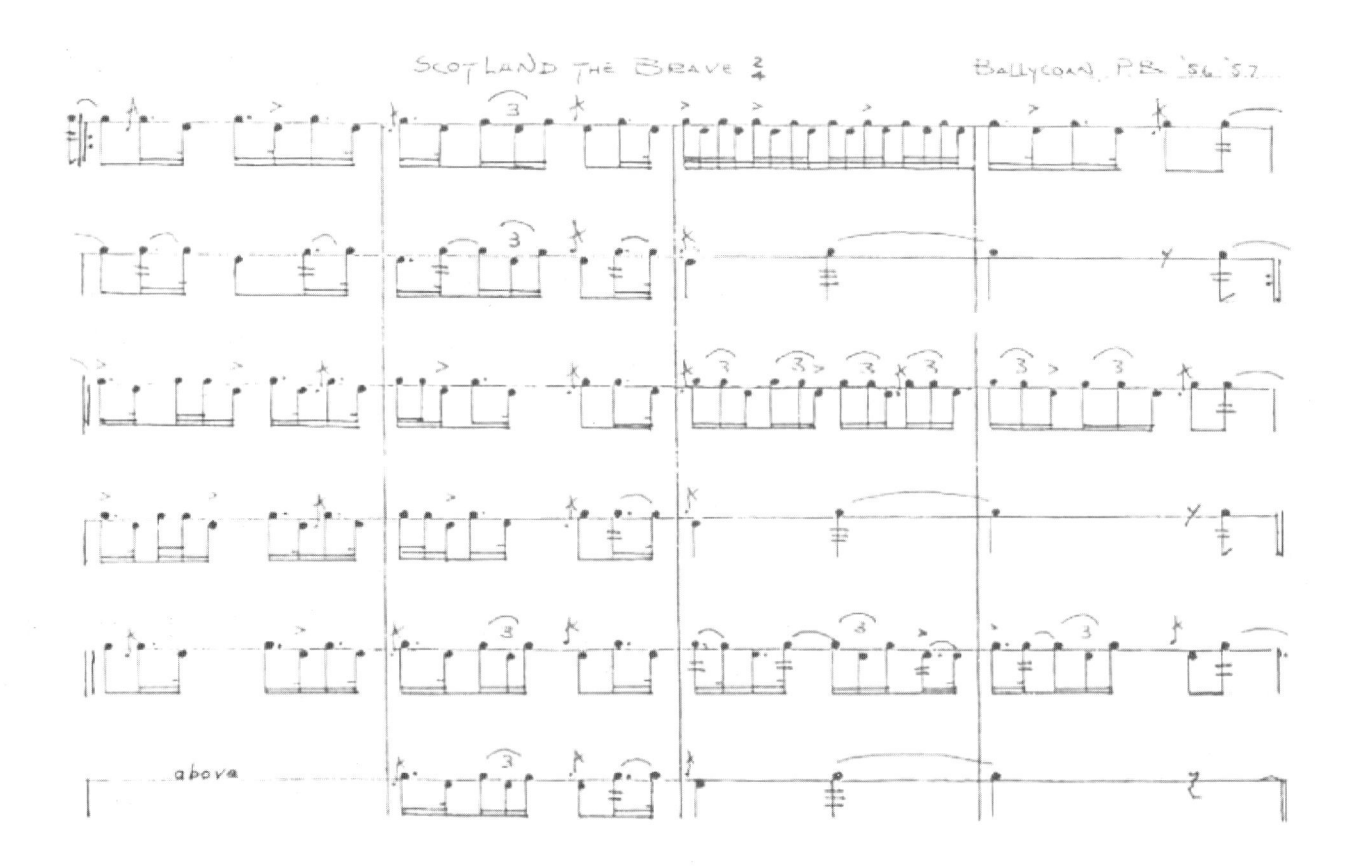

Scotland the Brave

Kit Reynolds 1956

2/4 March

Section 6

1960 - 1970
Influential Drummers

		Band	Featured Score	Page
Armit	Dave	Shotts & Dykehead	King George V's Army	**52**
Barnham	Billy	Robert Armstrong Memorial (NI)		
Barr	Bert	Shotts & Dykehead		
Boyd	Bert	Ayr		
Chatto	Allan	Sydney Thistle (Aus)		
Clark	Willie	Clan MacRae Society		
Connell	Alex	Glasgow City Police		
Docherty	Alex	Worcester Kilties (USA)		
Duthart	Alex	Shotts & Dykehead		
Gibson	Frank	Ballycoan (NI)		
Hosie	Andy	Renfrew		
Hutton	Jim	Muirhead & Sons	Dugald McColl	**54**
Mackay	Tom	Muirhead & Sons		
Montgomery	Bob	Edinburgh City Police	Arthur Bignold	**56**
Noble	Joe	Renfrew		
Rea	Bobby	Ballycoan (NI)		
Reynolds	Kit	Ballycoan (NI)		
Stevenson	Billy	Shotts & Dykehead		
Turner	Robert	Muirhead & Sons		
Young	Wilson	Red Hackle	The Highland Wedding	**58**

DRUM MAJOR DAVE ARMIT
SHOTTS & DYKEHEAD CALEDONIA PIPE BAND
WORCESTER KILTIE PIPE BAND (USA)

Dave Armit was born in Wishaw, Scotland and was introduced to pipe bands at an early age, as many of his family were members of the Newmains and District Pipe Band. Dave received lessons from many noted drummers in his area, but the one who made the greatest impression on him was the late John Kirkwood. At the age of 10, Dave joined the Craigneuk Parish Juvenile Pipe Band and later joined the Newmains band, where under L/D John Kirkwood, he won the Scottish under 18 Solo Drumming Championship at the age of 13.

In early 1957 he joined the Shotts & Dykehead Caledonia Pipe Band where Alex Duthart after an absence from pipe bands, was now L/D. The members of the new corps at outset, were Alex Duthart, Bert Barr and Dave Armit, and they won the World Drumming Championship in that same year. Wilson Young then joined the drum corps, later followed by Billy Stevenson and Joe Logan. This was to be the start of a new pipe band drumming era and dynasty with a completely fresh approach. Shotts would go on to win the Worlds Grade One Drumming over the next seven years and Dave himself won the SPBA Adult Solo Drumming Championship in 1963.

Dave married in that year and decided in early 1964, to emigrate from Scotland to the USA where he had an offer to join the Worcester Kiltie Pipe Band. Already there were a number of his drumming friends there, so it was to be an easy transition.

There were many successes to come his way as Leading Drummer of the band. The Worcester Kiltie Pipe Band was one of the most successful Grade 1-pipe bands in the USA and Canada during the 1970's and 80's. The band also made a very enlightening trip to Scotland in 1964. They were very successful at a number of minor contests and were placed 6th in the Grade 1 Worlds Pipe Band Championships. Dave has now retired from active playing though he still tutors at workshops and seminars throughout North America.

King George V's Army

2/4 March
Dave Armit 1981

DRUM MAJOR JIM HUTTON
MUIRHEAD AND SONS
INVERGORDON DISTILLERS
EDINBURGH CITY POLICE
SHOTTS AND DYKEHEAD CALEDONIA

Jim Hutton was born in Wishaw Lanarkshire, and his tutor was John Duthart, the father of Alex Duthart. In 1947, Jim's first band was Craigneuk Parish Church Juvenile, and in 1949 he joined Muirhead and Sons under their Leading Drummer, Jimmy Gray.

When Jim was 17 years of age he moved to the City of Edinburgh Police where George Pryde was in command of the drum Corps.

Upon completion of his National Service in The Royal Air Force, Jim returned to Muirhead and Sons ----- this time as Leading Drummer. The band had many successes during this period, including winning the Worlds Championship in 1961, with Jim leading the drum corps.

In 1965 he moved to the Invergordon Distillers band to play in Alex Duthart's drum corps and when in 1968, Alex left the band to join Edinburgh City Police, Jim followed. He followed once again when in 1972, Alex returned to lead the Shotts and Dykehead drum corps. (Alex had previously led the Shotts corps from 1957 until 1965).

Jim continued in Shotts and Dykehead until 1986 when having played in Grade 1 bands for a total of 37 years, he decided retire. During his lengthy playing career, Jim Hutton had 8 World Champion band performances and also 3 World Solo Titles to his credit.

He has been a member of the RSPBA Panel of Adjudicators since 1962, and is still actively involved in this area.

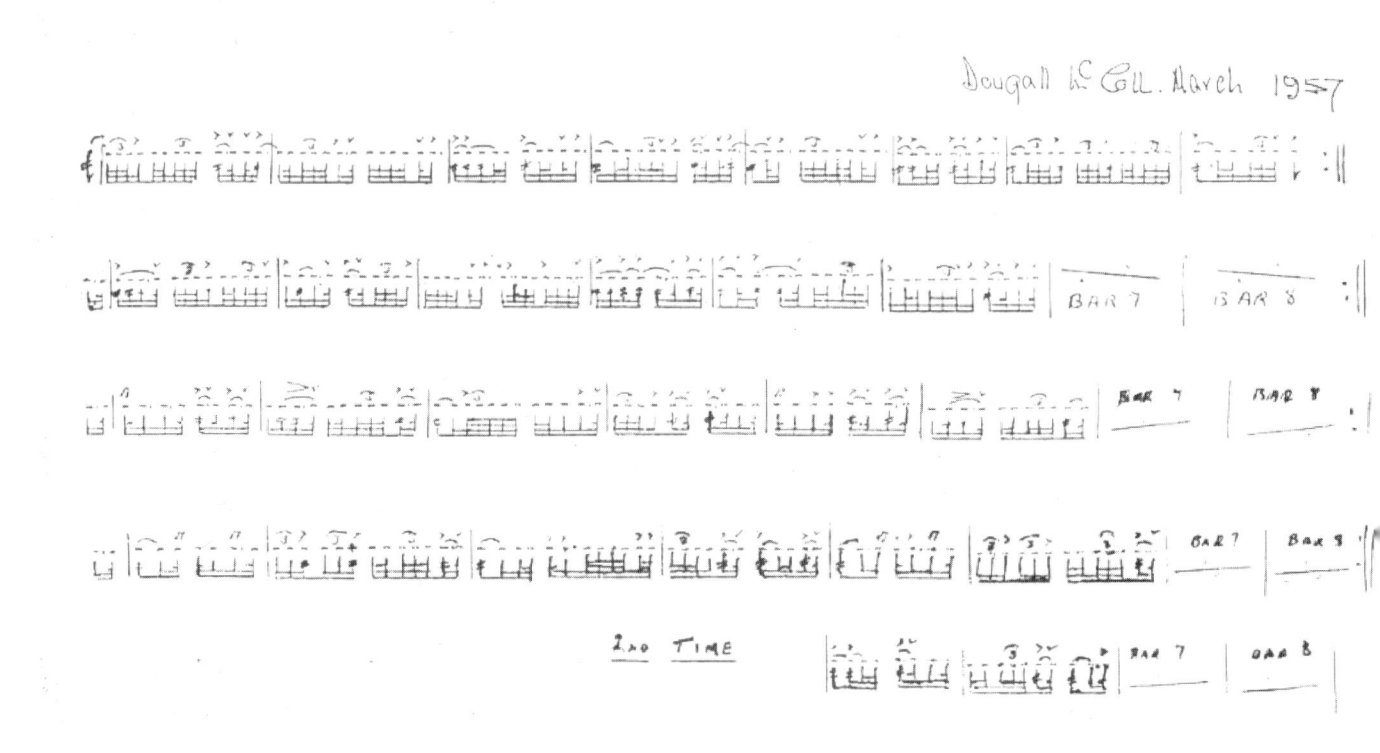

Dugald McColl

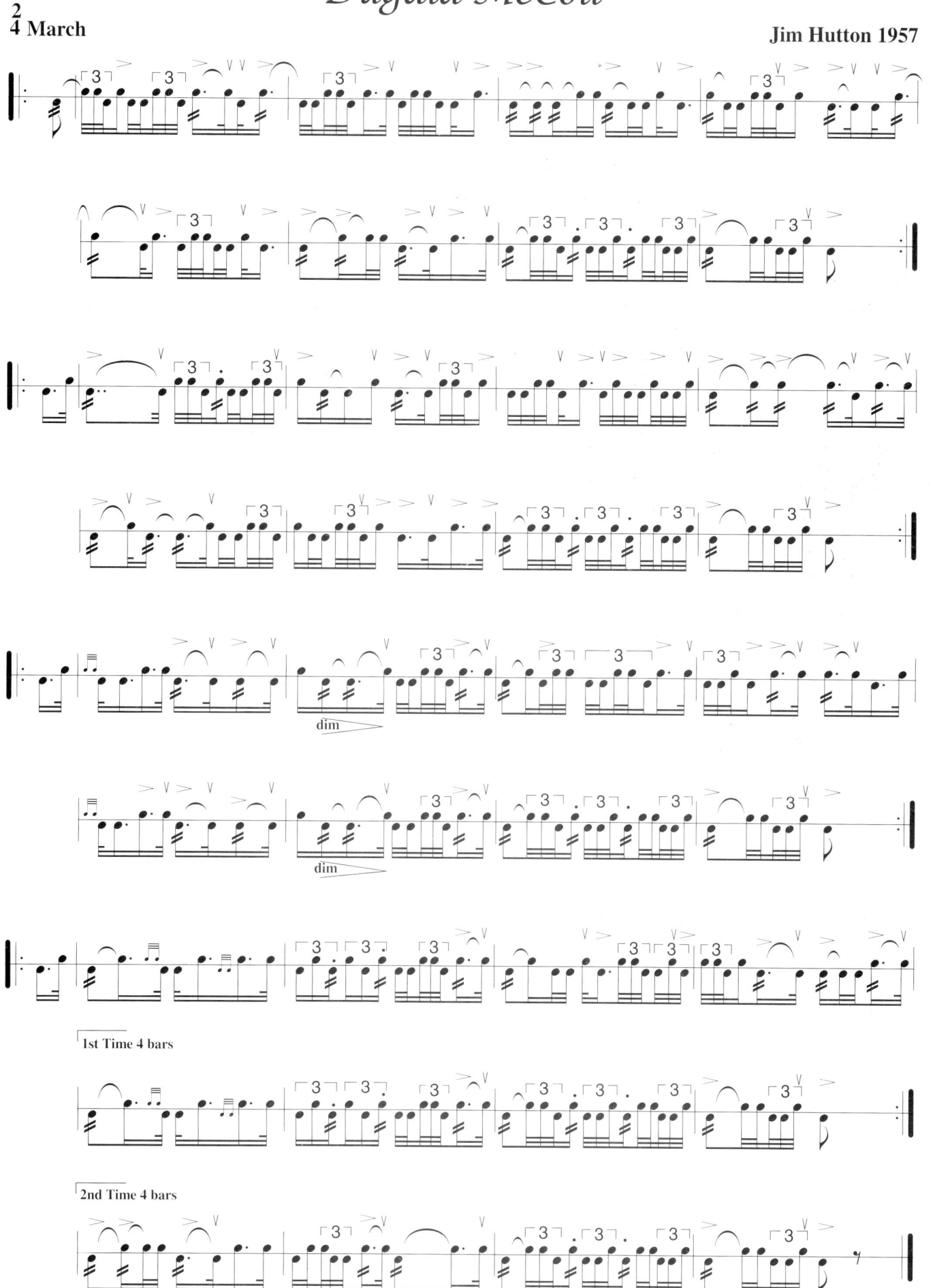

2/4 March

Jim Hutton 1957

DRUM MAJOR ROBERT (BOB) MONTGOMERY
EDINBURGH CITY POLICE PIPE BAND

Bob Montgomery was born in Greenock, Renfrewshire and started drumming at an early age. He initially played for a number of years with the Royal Naval Torpedo Factory Pipe Band. Later he joined the Greenock Police and played for a time with their pipe band. After a few years Bob decided to make the move to Edinburgh, joining *The Edinburgh City Police Pipe Band*. This was to be the start of a long and successful association with the band. Under his guidance the drum corps had many successes, with the band winning the Worlds Championships on no less than four occasions between 1963 and 1972. Bob's corps was also to win all the major drumming championship titles at least once, including in 1964, the Grade 1 Worlds Drumming. Bob corresponded regularly, exchanging his wide drumming knowledge with many drummers overseas. In major Solo Drumming competitions, he was regularly placed in the top three, including winning the Worlds Solo in 1962 and also in 1969. Over the years Bob, as holder of the RSPBA Advanced and the Ensemble Certification, was a regular tutor at Association Workshops and Clinics. He was also a qualified RSPBA Examiner, Lecturer and Adjudicator, and travelled overseas on many occasions representing the Association. In addition he tutored a number of school and college bands. Bob was a dedicated drummer and member of the pipe band movement. Sadly he passed away in 1997.

Arthur Bignold

Bob Montgomery 1969

2/4 March

DRUM MAJOR WILSON YOUNG
DALZELL HIGHLAND
SHOTTS & DYKEHEAD CALEDONIA PIPE BAND
THE RED HACKLE PIPES AND DRUMS

Wilson was born in Carluke, Lanarkshire where he first started playing in the local Boy Scout band under Guy Smith, their Leading Drummer. He later played with the Grade 2 Wishaw Highland Pipe Band. John Kirkwood (Senior) is listed as his first influential teacher.

Wilson progressed quickly and was invited in 1953 to join the Grade 1 **Dalzell Highland Pipe Band**, at that time under Leading Drummer, Billy Stevenson.

After a two-year stint doing National Service in the RAF, playing with Pipe, Military and Brass bands, Wilson was invited in late 1957, to join the newly formed corps of **Shotts & Dykehead Caledonia,** under **Alex Duthart**.

Following many successful years with the Shotts band winning 4 **Worlds Band** titles, 6 **Worlds Drumming** titles and 4 **Champion of Champions** titles, Wilson was invited to take over the position as Leading Drummer of the **Red Hackle Pipes and Drums**.

There, over the next 10 years, Wilson led his drum corps to win all Major titles with the exception of the Worlds. During this period the band were twice **Champion of Champions**.

As a Solo competitor, Wilson also made his mark, winning the SPBA **Worlds Solo** Championships in 1967 and was runner-up both in 1966 and in 1970.

Now retired, Wilson is a highly respected Adjudicator with the RSPBA. He has officiated throughout the UK and also in many other countries.

The Highland Wedding

March — Wilson Young 1967

Section 7

1970 - 1980
Influential Drummers

		Band	**Featured Score**	**Page**
Barr	Bert	Shotts & Dykehead		
Brown	Tom	Boghall & Bathgate	Donald MacLean's Farewell to Oban	**62**
Chatto	Allan	NSW Police (Aus)	Southall	**64**
Connell	Alex	Strathclyde Police	The Highland Wedding	**66**
Duthart	Alex	British Cal. Airways	John MacDonald of Glencoe	**68**
Hobbs	Wayne	City of Wellington (NZ)	The 74th's Farewell to Edinburgh	**70**
Hutton	Jim	Shotts & Dykehead		
Kilpatrick	Jim	Shotts & Dykehead		
King	James	Dysart & Dundonald	The Balmoral Highlanders	**72**
Lawrie	Doug	Queensland Police (Aus)		
Mac Innes	John	Pipers Whisky		
McErlean	Willie	Triumph St (Can.)		
Montgomery	Bob	Edinburgh City Police		
Noble	Joe	British Caledonian Renfrew	The Young MacGregor	**74**
Rea	Bobby	Royal Ulster Constabulary		
Scullion	John	Shotts & Dykehead		
Turner	Robert	Muirhead & Sons		
Young	Wilson	Red Hackle		

DRUM MAJOR TOM BROWN
SHOTTS & DYKEHEAD CALEDONIA PIPE BAND
BOGHALL & BATHGATE PIPE BAND

Tom Brown was born in Whitburn West Lothian, Scotland. When he was nine years old, he started learning the snare drum with the Whitrigg Colliery Pipe Band. Soon after, the band changed its name to the Polkemmet Colliery Pipe Band and Tom was later appointed Leading Drummer. This was to be the start of Tom's dedication to tutoring many youngsters, one of whom was his nephew Jim Kilpatrick.

Tom left Polkemmet in 1970 to join Alex Duthart in the Shotts Drum Corps, but he still continued his teaching classes producing many young champions. In 1977, Tom was invited to take over as L/D of Boghall & Bathgate Pipe Band. This was to be the start of an era that gave many major successes to the Boghall drum corps. In 1980, their first season in Grade 1, they gained 4th in the Worlds and 'placings' in many other 'Majors'. By 1982, Tom's "bairns" were to win their second Worlds Drumming Championship and many other successes were to follow. Tom's son and daughter were now also playing in the Grade I Drum Corps.

The Boghall unit then created two new Juvenile bands and also a Grade 2 band. Tom and P/M Robert Martin were deeply committed and involved in tutoring all of these bands.

Today we can see the value of the tuition, there still being **four** Boghall bands, all featuring in many of the prize lists at competitions. Tom has now "retired" as L/D of the big band, but plays L/D with the Grade 2 corps. There his successes include two World Championships and the corps has been Champion of Champions these last 3-4 years. His son Gordon is presently the L/D of the Grade 1 band.

Tom continues to be as busy as ever with his 'Drumming Academy" and conducting Drumming Workshops and Seminars in countries throughout the world, such as Canada and the USA, Australia and New Zealand, Holland and Belgium.

Donald MacLean's Farewell to Oban

March
Tom Brown 1992

DRUM MAJOR ALLAN CHATTO
INVERCARGILL (NZ)　　　　RUTHERGLEN (Scot)
SYDNEY THISTLE (Aus)　　NSW POLICE (Aus)

Allan, born in Sydney, Australia in 1932, started his pipe band drumming career early in 1948 with the local St George Pipe Band. A keen student of music, in his early years Allan corresponded with Drum Major Jack Seton of the famous Glasgow Police Pipe Band.

In 1952, Allan, keen to expand his drumming knowledge, travelled to New Zealand where he joined the Invercargill Pipe Band under Leading Drummer Jim Kirkpatrick (ex Ballycoan N.I.). The band were NZ Champions that year. In 1954, Allan was appointed Leading Drummer.

In 1956 Allan left for Scotland where he joined the Glasgow Transport P.B., playing the rest of the season with their Grade 1 Drum Corps. He studied for the SPBA Drumming College Examinations and gained both the Elementary and the Advanced Certificate. The next season saw him playing with the Rutherglen P.B. Drum Corps, again in Grade 1 under L/D Willie Corr. Allan remained with Rutherglen until he married and returned to Australia in late 1959.

There he joined the Sydney Thistle Highland Pipe Band as Leading Drummer. He had many successes during the 1960's, winning National and State championships. Allan was a very successful solo competitor winning many Australian and State Championships

In 1976, he was invited to the NSW Police Pipe Band as Leading Drummer. The band and drum corps were very successful. Allan continued with the band until 1989.

Allan then retired from active playing but continued to tutor and adjudicate. He was appointed to the RSPBA Adjudication Panel in 1986. Since then he has adjudicated at a number of competitions in Scotland, including the Worlds on three occasions. Allan has also adjudicated at a number of National Championships in Australia and New Zealand.

During his career Allan has been appointed to many positions within the NSWPBA including Vice Principal Drumming. Later, he was appointed Principal of Drumming for the AFPBA, a position he held for over 25 years. He also was deeply involved in establishing a pipe band Drumming Course in the Escola de Gaitas de Ourense, Galicia in Spain.

Upon retirement, Allan has maintained his worldwide drumming correspondence, exchanging music and drum scores with drummers in many countries. He has written a number of tutor books on pipe band drumming and lectured in many countries. Allan is a well-respected Drumming Adjudicator at home in Australia and also overseas.

"SOUTH HALL" 2/4 March

"Southall"

$\frac{2}{4}$ March

Allan Chatto 1988

DRUM MAJOR ALEX CONNELL
RENFREW PIPE BAND
STRATHCLYDE POLICE PIPE BAND

In 1947 Alex Connell started his drumming career with the 214 Company of the Glasgow Boys Brigade.

At the age of 18 years he was appointed to the position of Leading Drummer in the Renfrew Pipe Band where his corps was successful in winning the European Drumming Championship at Belfast.

In 1958 Alex joined the Glasgow Police and in January 1961, became Drum Sergeant of their band. During his time with the Police, they were renamed *"The Strathclyde Police Pipe Band"*.

The successes of this famous pipe band are world known. They were Worlds champions many times, also RSPBA Champion of Champions on many occasions. In 1972 they also won the Worlds Drumming championship, but probably the Drum Corps finest year was 1981 when they won the Scottish, European and Cowal Championships.

In Solo drumming competitions, Alex won both the Junior and Senior Boys Brigade Championships. As an adult, he won the Glasgow and West of Scotland Solo Championships many times. During his successful career in the 1960 – 70's Alex was rarely out of the top six placing's in the RSPBA Worlds Solo Drumming Championships.

We feature part of Alex's original score for the competition 2/4 March "The Highland Wedding"

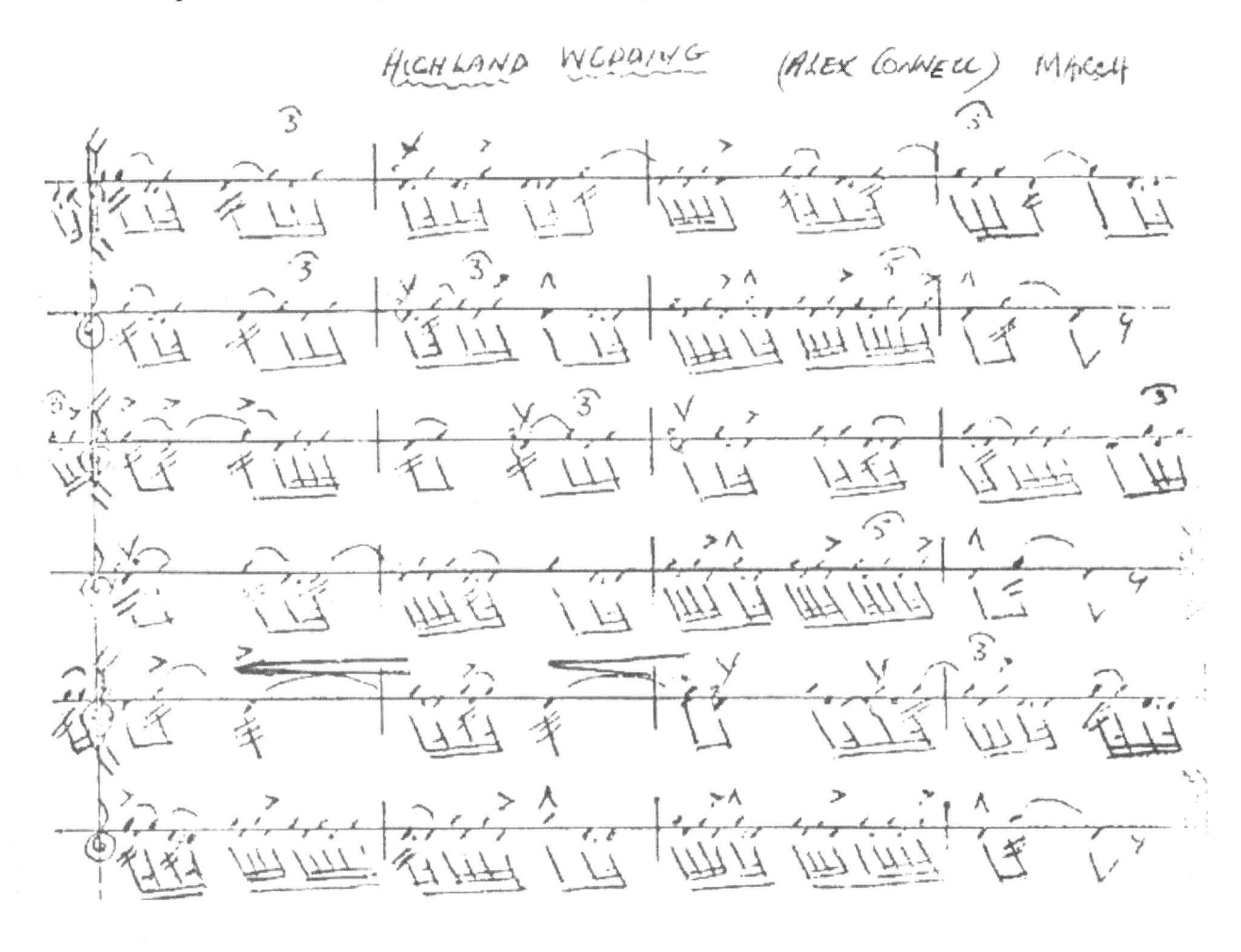

The Highland Wedding

2/4 March
Alex Connell 1980

DRUM MAJOR ALEX DUTHART
CRAIGNEUK PARISH PIPE BAND
DALZELL HIGHLAND PIPE BAND
SHOTTS & DYKEHEAD CALEDONIA PIPE BAND
INVERGORDON DISTILLERS PIPE BAND
EDINBURGH CITY POLICE PIPE BAND
BRITISH CALEDONIAN AIRWAYS PIPE BAND

Following his many successes with the Shotts and Dykehead Caledonia Pipe Band, Alex was to lead the drum corps of some other famous Grade 1 bands. These included Invergordon Distillers, Edinburgh City Police and finally the British Caledonian Airways pipe band. Once again Alex and his various Corps had many successes. He set the standard for other drum corps to follow, and a new era in pipe band drumming was established.

Alex also visited many countries to adjudicate and to lecture on pipe band drumming. He was a "master of his art" and musicians in other music idioms have been greatly influenced by his playing style, control and technique.

It is impossible to list all of Alex's achievements and contributions to drumming. The pipe band world was deeply saddened by his untimely death while playing in New York City with the British Caledonian Airways band in November 1986.

He was a wonderful pipe band drummer but recognised by musicians skilled in other types of music too. A modest man admired by everyone who knew him.

A sample of one of Alex's great scores from the 1970 – 80's era is shown below.

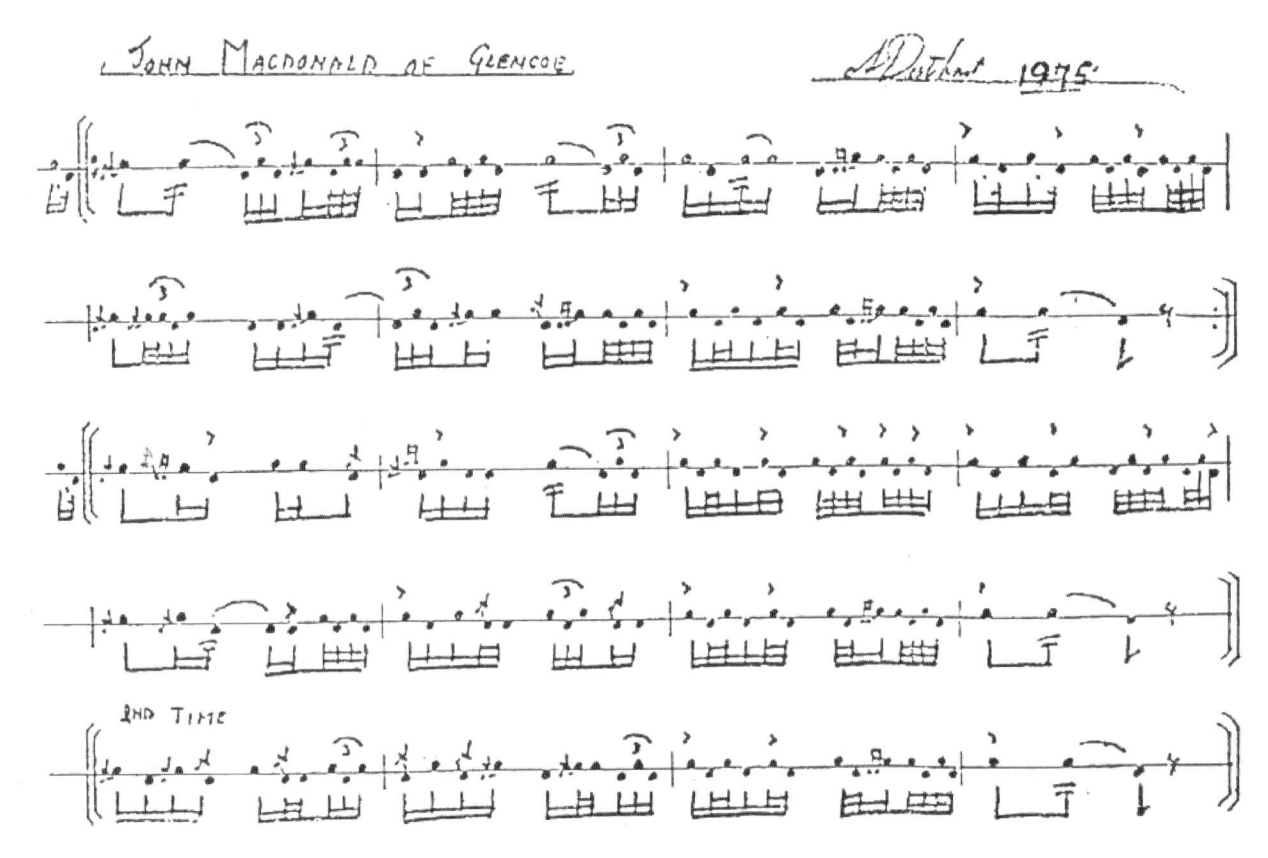

John MacDonald of Glencoe

2/4 March

Alex Duthart 1975

N.B. Drag movements played in pipe bands are generally of the closed variety and should be written with their stems drawn in an upwards direction showing a slur leading to the main note.
However, very often the practice has been to omit the slur but still play the drag closed.
Great care should be taken when playing the above score. It contains not only a mixture of both closed and open drags, but sometimes a flam is also played on the 1st note of the open drag.
At a later date Alex signified an open drag by showing the stems drawn in a downwards direction. (WY)

DRUM MAJOR WAYNE HOBBS
CITY OF WELLINGTON PIPE BAND (N.Z.)
RENFREW PIPE BAND

Wayne Hobbs was born in 1947 in New Zealand. At an early age he took an interest in drumming, his first band being the Tawa & District where he mastered the basics. In 1964, Wayne moved to the City of Wellington under L/D Eric Skachill. He progressed quickly. In his first Grade 1 NZ Championships the corps came 2nd. The following three years they were placed NZ Grade 1 Drumming Champions.

By 1970, Wayne felt that he had progressed as far as he could in NZ, so left by ship for Scotland. There he went for private lessons with the well-known A.D.Hamilton. Shortly after "AD" introduced him to Joe Noble, L/D with the Renfrew Pipe Band, who invited him to come and join the band. In a little over three months Wayne had learned the contest scores and was a member of the Drum Corps which won the European title in 1970 & 71, then 3rd place in the Worlds in 71. Also in 1971, the band won the Cowal Drumming Championship. The last few months before Wayne returned home to NZ in late 1971, he spent learning new techniques under Alex Duthart and the Shotts Drum corps.

On returning home, he took over the City of Wellington corps as L/D and over the next 15 or so years his corps was rarely beaten in competition. The band also made several successful trips to Australia. Wayne Hobbs was a very consistent and successful solo player. Later he moved to live in Auckland where he took over the American Airlines drum corps which made several trips to Scotland competing in Grade 1. Wayne has also held the position as Principal of the RNZPBA Drumming College for a number of years. He has contributed greatly to pipe band drumming in N.Z.

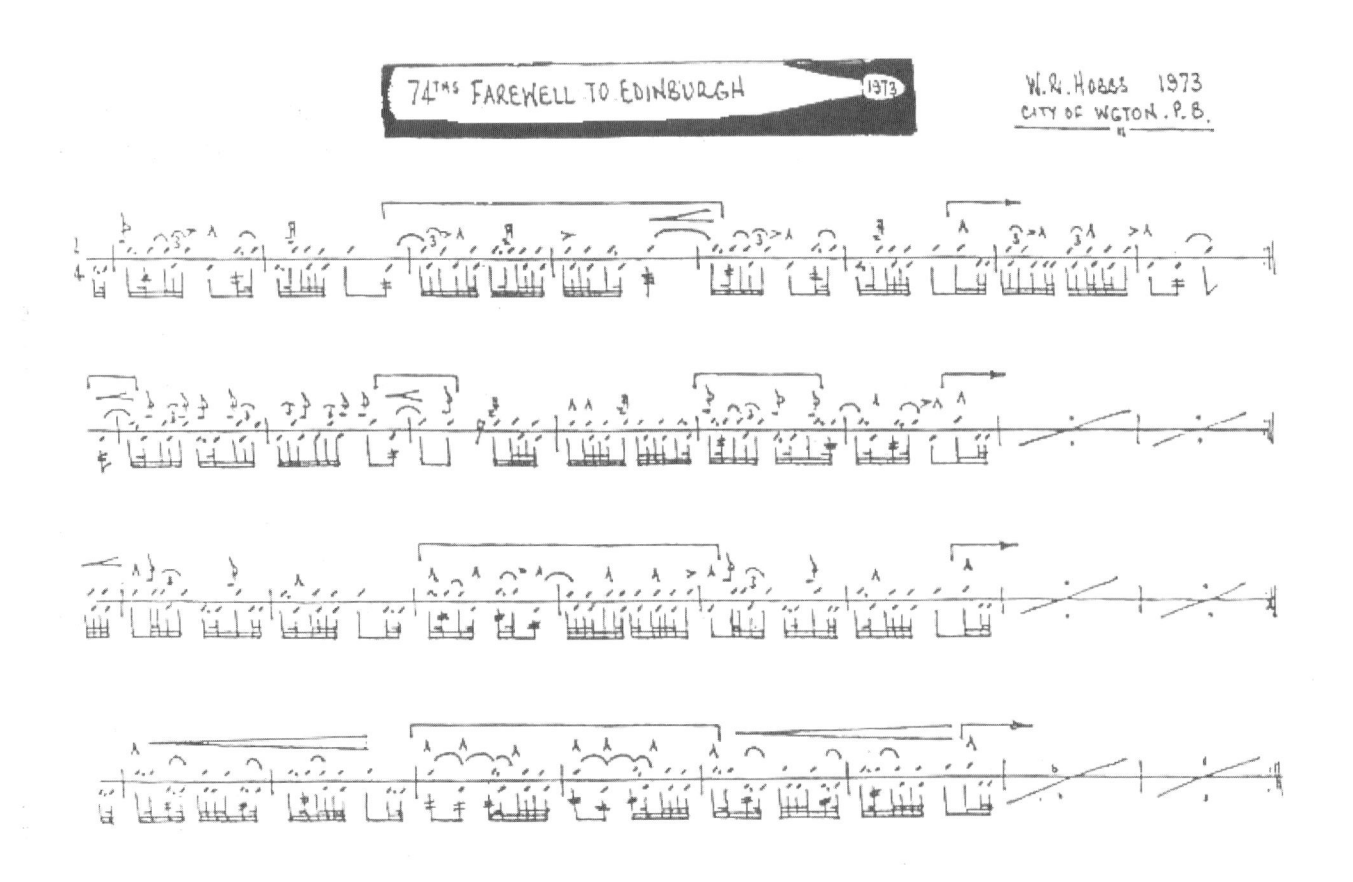

The 74ths Farewell to Edinburgh

$\frac{2}{4}$ March

Wayne Hobbs 1973

DRUM MAJOR JAMES KING
DYSART AND DUNDONALD PIPE BAND
POLKEMMET GRORUD PIPE BAND
MCNAUGHTONS VALE OF ATHOLL PIPE BAND

James has been a successful player these past 26 years and from the start of his career he has been viewed as an innovator. He has always provided imaginative and interesting scores for the bands in which he has served as leading Drummer.

In his early career, James was leading Drummer with Dysart and Dundonald and led his Corps to many Grade 1 titles including four World Championships.

In the mid 1980's he joined forces with another 'JK' (Jim Kilpatrick) in the Polkemmet band and helped the Corps to a number of successes.

Following a two-year break in the USA (still involved in drumming), James and P/M David Barnes took over the leadership of Polkemmet. The year 1991 was a memorable one as the band won its first ever Major Title.

In 1992, James joined The Vale of Atholl and since then the band and Drum Corps have enjoyed many successes in Grade 1. One of his more recent compositions is featured below.

The Balmoral Highlanders

2/4 March
James King 1998

DRUM MAJOR JOE NOBLE
RENFREW PIPE BAND

Born in Fraserburgh, Aberdeenshire. Joe started playing at age 12 with the 214th Glasgow Company of the Boys Brigade. This was a very successful Juvenile pipe band and all major Juvenile Titles were won, on many occasions. His drum tutors at this time were Alex Helie and George Hunter. The Pipe Major of the 214 was Alex McIver whom Joe states probably had the greatest influence on his playing style.

He joined Renfrew Pipe Band in 1960 and took over as Leading Drummer in 1965. This Band changed it's name as a result of sponsorship deals firstly to British Caledonian Airways (Renfrew) Band and then to Babcock Renfrew Pipe Band.

Shortly after taking over the leading drum position at Renfrew he was fortunate to meet Alex D. Hamilton, a top percussionist, who also influenced his drumming career greatly.

Joe moved to Toyota Pipes & Drums in 1983 and to The City of Glasgow in 1989. He retired from playing in 1991 having played for 35 years. (28 of these as Leading Drummer within various bands and 30 years in Grade 1.)

Drum corps' under his direction have won several prizes including all Major Grade 1 titles, i.e. Scottish, British, European, Cowal and World Championships.

Overall, he has accepted trophies on behalf of various drum corps over a period of 35yrs spread within each of the 5 decades, 1950's-90's.

In the Solo field he has enjoyed many successes, including two first places in the World Solo Drumming Competition. He was the first winner of the official 'World Solo Drumming Championship' (previously known as the SPBA-later RSPBA, Solo Drumming Championship.)

Since retiring from playing, Joe has been an active member of the RSPBA Panel of Adjudicators.

The Young MacGregor

2/4 March

Joe Noble 1969

Section 8

1980 - 1999
Influential Drummers

		Band	Featured Score	Page
Brown	Gordon	Boghall & Bathgate	John MacDonald of Glencoe	78
Brown	Tom	Boghall & Bathgate		
Collins	Jim	Glasgow Skye Association		
Cook	Arthur	Lothian & Borders Police	The Balmoral Highlanders	80
Corkin	Gary	Royal Ulster Constabulary(NI)		
Craig	Allan	Glasgow Skye Association		
Craig	Gordon	Glasgow Skye Association		
Cranston	Neil	Boghall & Bathgate		
Dawson	Harvey	78th Fraser Highlanders(Can.)		
Duthart	Alex	British Caledonian Airways		
Gillespie	Harold	Victoria Police(Aus.)	The Conundrum	82
Houlden	Jackie	Babcock Renfrew		
Hunter	Michael	78th Fraser Highlanders(Can.)		
Kerr	Willie	Shotts & Dykehead		
Kilpatrick	Jim	Shotts & Dykehead	Donald MacLean's Farewell to Oban	84
King	Jim	Vale of Atholl		
Kirkwood	John(Jnr)	Strathclyde Police	Michael Grey	86
Maxwell	Reid	Simon Fraser Univ.(Can.)	Tom Wilson	88
Noble	Joe	The City of Glasgow		
Parkes	Gordon	F/M Montgomery(NI)	The Highland Wedding	90
Rea	Bobby	Ravara (NI)		
Scullion	Andy	Cullybackey(NI)		
Scullion	John	Scottish Power	Beaumont Hamel	92
Turner	Paul	Vale of Atholl	John McMillan of Barra	94
Ward	Eric	Strathclyde Police	The Balmoral Highlanders	96
Walls	George	The City of Glasgow		
Wilson	Barry	Shotts & Dykehead		

DRUM MAJOR GORDON BROWN

BOGHALL AND BATHGATE PIPE BAND

Born in Whitburn - West Lothian, Gordon was taught by his father Tom Brown. At the age of twelve he joined the Boghall & Bathgate Caledonia Novice Juvenile Pipe Band. He enjoyed a successful period in the Juvenile ranks as a soloist and drum corps member within the Band. Gordon left the Juvenile Band in 1978 to join his father who was Leading Drummer of Boghall & Bathgate Caledonia, which had just been newly promoted to Grade 2.

The Band was upgraded to Grade 1 in 1980 and the Drum Corps enjoyed a highly successful run winning all the major titles including three consecutive World titles 1981, 1982 and 1983.

During this period Gordon won two World Juvenile Solo titles.

In 1991, Gordon succeeded his father as Leading Drummer of the Band and to date has led them to many major titles.

Gordon has also enjoyed a number of successes in Adult Solo competitions and these include winning the World Solo Drumming Championship in 1994.

John MacDonald of Glencoe

2/4 March
Gordon Brown 1993

DRUM MAJOR ARTHUR COOK
SHOTTS & DYKEHEAD CALEDONIA PIPE BAND
LOTHIAN & BORDERS POLICE PIPE BAND

Arthur Cook was born in Bellshill, Lanarkshire, Scotland. When he was eleven years old, Arthur started playing the snare drum with the Stonehouse Pipe Band. He later joined the Larkhall British Legion Pipe Band.

Encouraged to further his drumming skills, at the age of sixteen Arthur joined the Shotts & Dykehead Caledonia Pipe Band. There he was under the guidance of Drum Major Alex Duthart.

He later joined the British Caledonian Airways Drum Corps. Arthur was with B Cal Pipe Band with Alex and some other members of the former Shotts corps for three years until the sudden passing of Alex Duthart. Arthur was then to return to Shotts as Leading Drummer. One year later he was to return to the B Cal Corps.

In 1987, Arthur joined the Lothian & Borders Police Pipe Band as Leading Drummer and for a number of years he led his corps to numerous successes. He then played for a short period with the BT Polkemmet band before returning once more to lead the Police band.

Arthur is a prolific Solo Drumming prizewinner and his successes include five times winner of the Lothian & Borders Branch Solos. He has gained a number of placings in the World's Solo Drumming Championships. In 1988 Arthur was the RSPBA World Solo Drumming Champion.

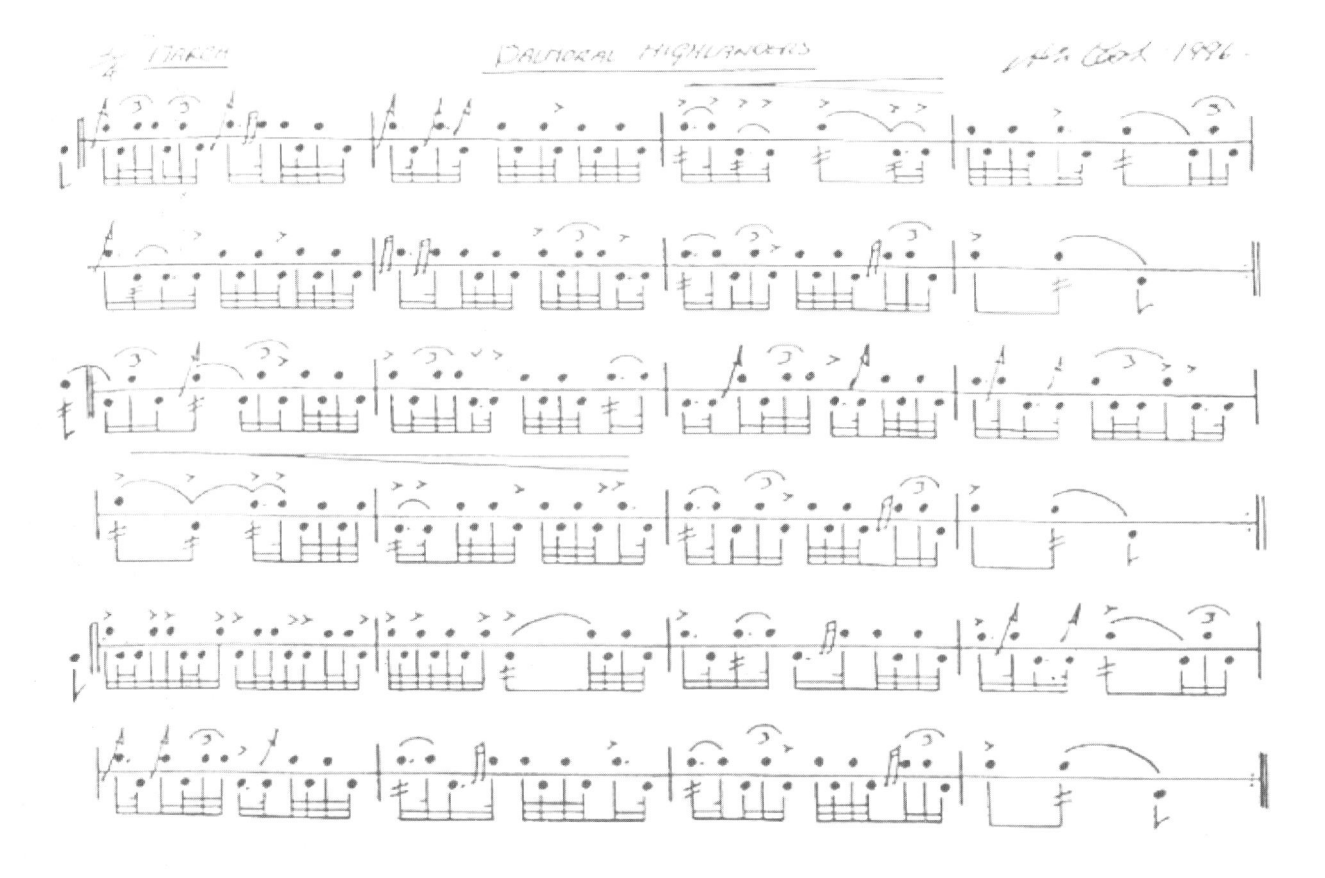

The Balmoral Highlanders

March   **Arthur Cook 1996**

DRUM MAJOR HAROLD GILLESPIE
NUNAWADING PIPE BAND (AUS.)
VICTORIA POLICE PIPE BAND (AUS.)

Born in Belfast, Northern Ireland, Harold emigrated to Australia in 1954 at the age of two.

He began his drumming career at age nine with Mitcham Pipe Band. He later joined Nunawading Pipe Band where in his early teens he successfully led the drum corps to two consecutive Australian Championships. Also in his teenage years, Harold was successful in Solo Competitions winning both the Juvenile and Senior Solo titles at State and National Championships.

At the age of 16, Harold returned to Northern Ireland where he further developed his technical skills under the guidance of Jackie Gamble of the Ballynahinch Pipe Band. The time spent in the U.K allowed Harold invaluable access to the worlds best pipe band drummers.

The knowledge he had gained was put into good use upon his return to Australia in 1975, where he became influential in the development of drumming in the State of Victoria and in particular with Hawthorn and Nunawading Pipe Bands.

In 1987 Harold joined the Victoria Police and developed Australia's most successful drum corps. Influenced by Andrew Scullion and Paul Turner, Harold has guided the Victoria Police drum corps for 10 years, where they remain undefeated in competition in the Southern Hemisphere.

The Victoria Police Pipe Band won the 1998 World Championships and the drum corps were 2nd place runners-up.

Harold is Vice-Principal for Drumming and a long serving member of the APBA Panel of Drumming Adjudicators. His services as an instructor are continually sought throughout Australia and also in other countries.

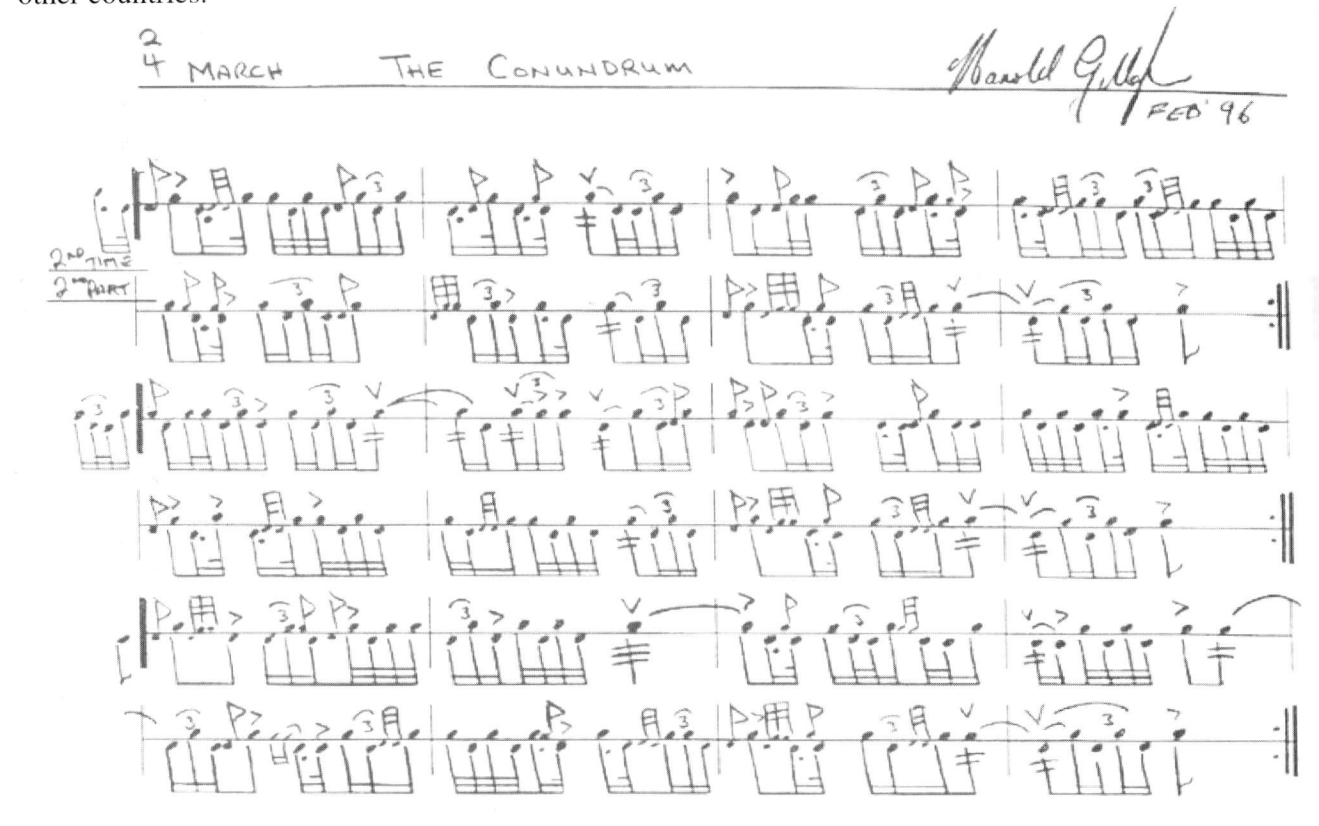

The Conundrum

2/4 March
Harold Gillespie 1996

N.B.
In this score, all drags with upward stems are played closed.
Drags with downward stems are played open. (WY)

DRUM MAJOR JIM KILPATRICK
SHOTTS & DYKEHEAD CALEDONIA PIPE BAND
POLKEMMET GRORUD PIPE BAND

JIM KILPATRICK started playing drums at the age of ten. His progress was so rapid that within two years he was competing at the highest level in Grade 1.

It was at the age of fifteen that Jim won his first Worlds Drum Corps Championships with the Shotts and Dykehead band led by the legendary Alex Duthart. This was to be the first of Jim's sixteen World Drum Corps titles. Twelve of these were won as a leading drummer and include winning the 1998 Drum Corps Championship for a record breaking eleven times in a row. Also in 1998, Jim's drum corps were crowned (once again) **"Champion of Champions"**. This set another record of 10 times ----- 9 of them consecutively.

Jim's move into the solo drumming arena proved to be equally successful. He has won the World Solo Drumming Championships a record eleven times in the course of his drumming career.

He has won every major championship including "Champion of Champions", in the Pipe Band, in the Drum Corps, and as a Soloist.

Jim has worked for Premier Percussion for twenty years and he was deeply involved in the development of the Tendura head and the world famous HTS 200 and HTS 700 snare drums.

Jim's talent and reputation are such that he has been invited to teach in schools all over the world as well as making countless appearances at drum clinics and festivals. These have included The Royal School of Music (London & Glasgow), and The Percussion Arts Society International Convention in the USA. Jim has received one of the highest accolades in drumming, by being presented with the "Life Time Achievement Award" for drumming by the Percussion Arts Society.

These achievements rank JIM KILPATRICK as one of the top percussionists in the world today and he is regarded as the world's greatest exponent of the snare drum.

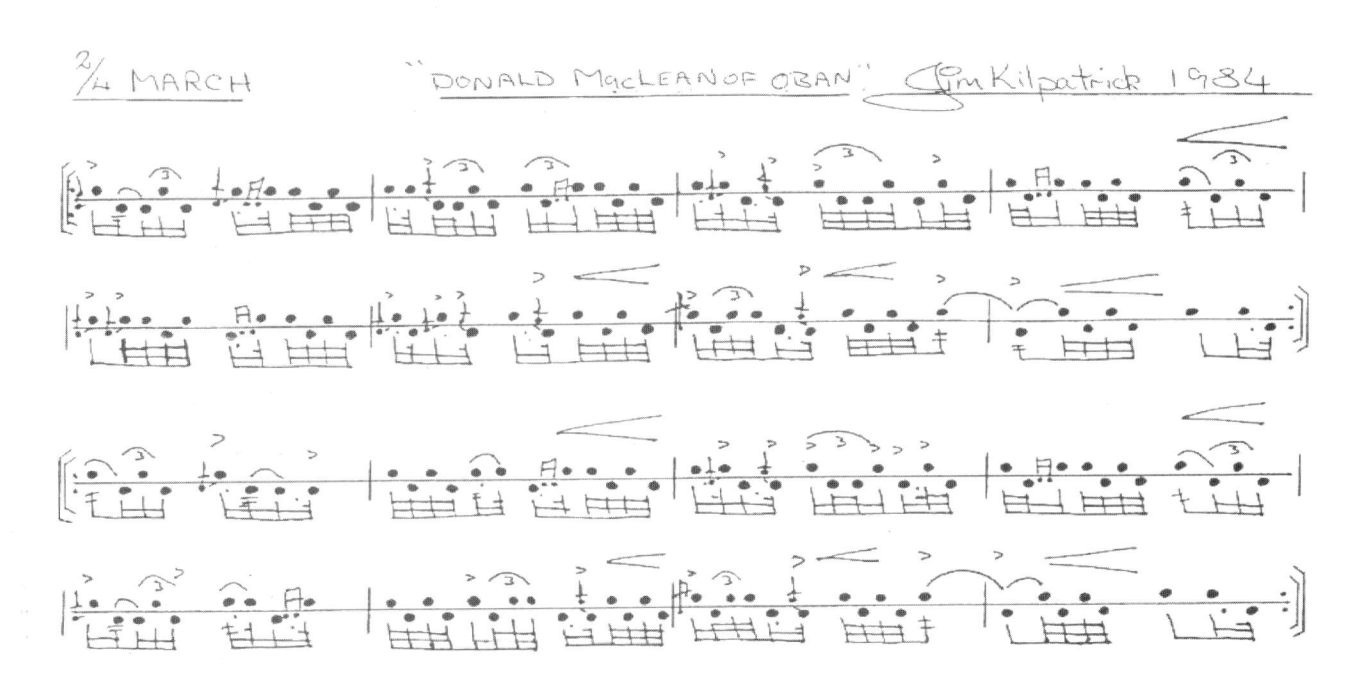

2/4 MARCH   "DONALD MacLEAN OF OBAN"   Jim Kilpatrick 1984

Donald MacLean's Farewell to Oban

$\frac{2}{4}$ March

Jim Kilpatrick 1984

DRUM MAJOR JOHN KIRKWOOD (Jnr.)
CLAN MACFARLANE PIPE BAND (CAN.)
THE STRATHCLYDE POLICE PIPE BAND

John Kirkwood was born in St Catharines, Canada. He is the son of John Kirkwood the former L/D of Shotts & Dykehead Caledonia Pipe Band and John (Jnr.) was destined to follow his father in a successful drumming career. He began learning at an early age under the guidance of his father and it was not long before he was playing in the drum corps of the Clan MacFarlane Pipe Band where John Snr. was L/D.

John Kirkwood (Jnr.) went on to win the Canadian and North American Solo Drumming Championships.

In 1977, in an effort to improve his drumming knowledge, John moved to Scotland and joined the famous Muirhead & Sons Pipe Band, under P/M Robert Hardie and L/D Robert Turner.

John played in the drum corps for two seasons and he also studied piping under Bob Hardie.

He returned to Canada in 1979, but missed the Scottish band scene.

In 1982, having been invited by D/M Alex Connell, he decided to return to Scotland where in 1983 he joined the drum corps of the Strathclyde Police Pipe Band.

John played in the corps for three years until Alex Connell's retiral when he took over as Leading Drummer for the 1986 'season'. Many successes followed.

In the 7 years when John was L/D of the band, Strathclyde Police won 18 Pipe Band Championship competitions, 5 Worlds, 4 Cowal, 4 European, 4 British and 1 Scottish championship.

Sadly the great combination of P/M Ian McLellan and L/D John Kirkwood was not to continue.

In 1992 ill health forced John's retiral both from the Strathclyde Police force and from the band.

A great personality and drummer, he has contributed much to the pipe band movement.

Michael Grey

Michael Grey

John Kirkwood (Jnr) 1990

2/4 March

DRUM MAJOR J. REID MAXWELL
DYSART AND DUNDONALD
78TH FRASER HIGHLANDERS (CAN.)
SIMON FRASER UNIVERSITY (CAN.)

J Reid Maxwell is without a doubt one of today's most decorated lead drummers. When the Simon Fraser University Pipe Band captured "the Worlds" in 1995 and more recently in 1999, Reid became the first person in history to lead the drum corps of two different bands to win the World Pipe Band Championship (his other victory was in 1987 with the 78th Fraser Highlanders). In addition to his band successes, in 1987 and again in 1999 his Drum Corps were also World Champions.

Reid began his drumming career at age five under the instruction of William Bell and the Ballingry School Pipe Band, the junior band of the Dysart & Dundonald Pipe Band. He eventually became lead drummer and then graduated to the Dysart band at age fourteen. With Dysart & Dundonald, he won two World Pipe Band Championships and four World Drum Corps Championships.

During the 1980s Reid emigrated to Canada, where he has continued his winning streak; with SFU's 1999 win, Reid obtained his eleventh World Championship.

As a solo competitor, Reid has won every major drumming prize in North America several times and three times placed in the top five at the World Solo Drumming Championships. In addition, Reid is a tireless composer, adjudicator and instructor, and is the driving force behind SFU's junior program, the Robert Malcolm Memorial Pipe Band. His ability to produce exceptional drum corps and his dedication to the instruction of young drummers is held in high regard worldwide.

March — Tom Wilson — J. Reid Maxwell Nov-16th-1994

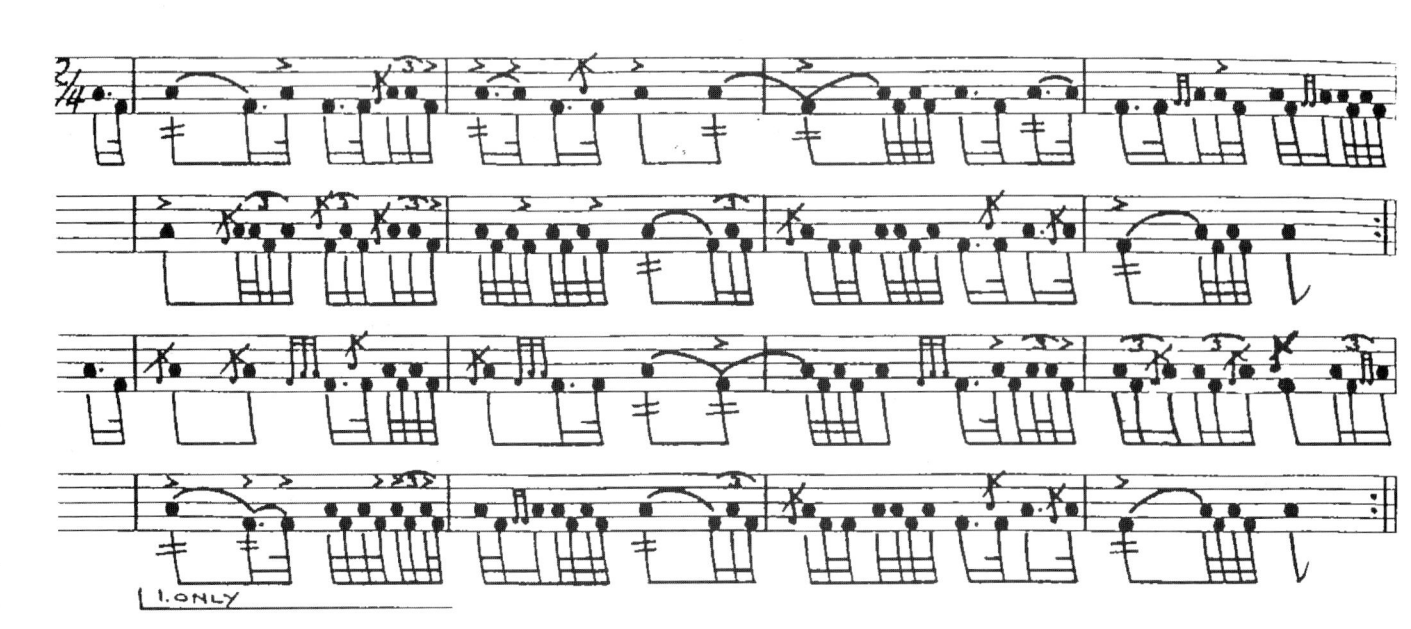

Tom Wilson

2/4 March — J. Reid Maxwell 1994

DRUM MAJOR GORDON PARKES
FIELD MARSHALL MONTGOMERY PIPE BAND

Gordon Parkes was the Leading Drummer of the Field Marshall Montgomery Pipe Band of Carryduff, Northern Ireland. When he joined the band in the early 1970's, they were in Grade 3. Gordon's first tutor was John Rea, who was for some time L/D of the Robert Armstrong Memorial Pipe Band. During Gordon's first 13/14 years he learned drumming by the "rote" method. Later he was to join the N.I. Piping and Drumming School and study the RSPBA College Examination requirements. This was to open a new perspective to his drumming.

In 1981 Gordon took over the 'Field Marshall' drum corps as L/D.

Having progressed quickly through the lower grades, by 1987 the band had been elevated to the RSPBA Grade 1 level.

Since that time the Field Marshall Montgomery has dominated pipe band competitions in Northern Ireland. In Scotland they have won the Worlds Grade 1 Pipe Band Championship on two occasions, 1992 and 1993. The band was also RSPBA Champion of Champions in the same years. They have won all of the Major RSPBA championships on at least one occasion, and have rarely been out of the top six places.

The Field Marshall Montgomery band has been N.I. and All Ireland Champions on a number of occasions, and the drum corps has been equally successful over the last 10 years.

Gordon, the holder the RSPBA Advanced Certificate, is a highly respected Drumming Adjudicator. He has officiated in Scotland and Northern Ireland and also in several overseas countries. He has been invited to visit a number of countries as a Tutor to conduct Drumming Workshops and Seminars. In 1998 after 18 years as L/D of the band, Gordon felt that he had to resign due to heavy work commitments. When time permits, he still plays with the drum corps on occasional outings.

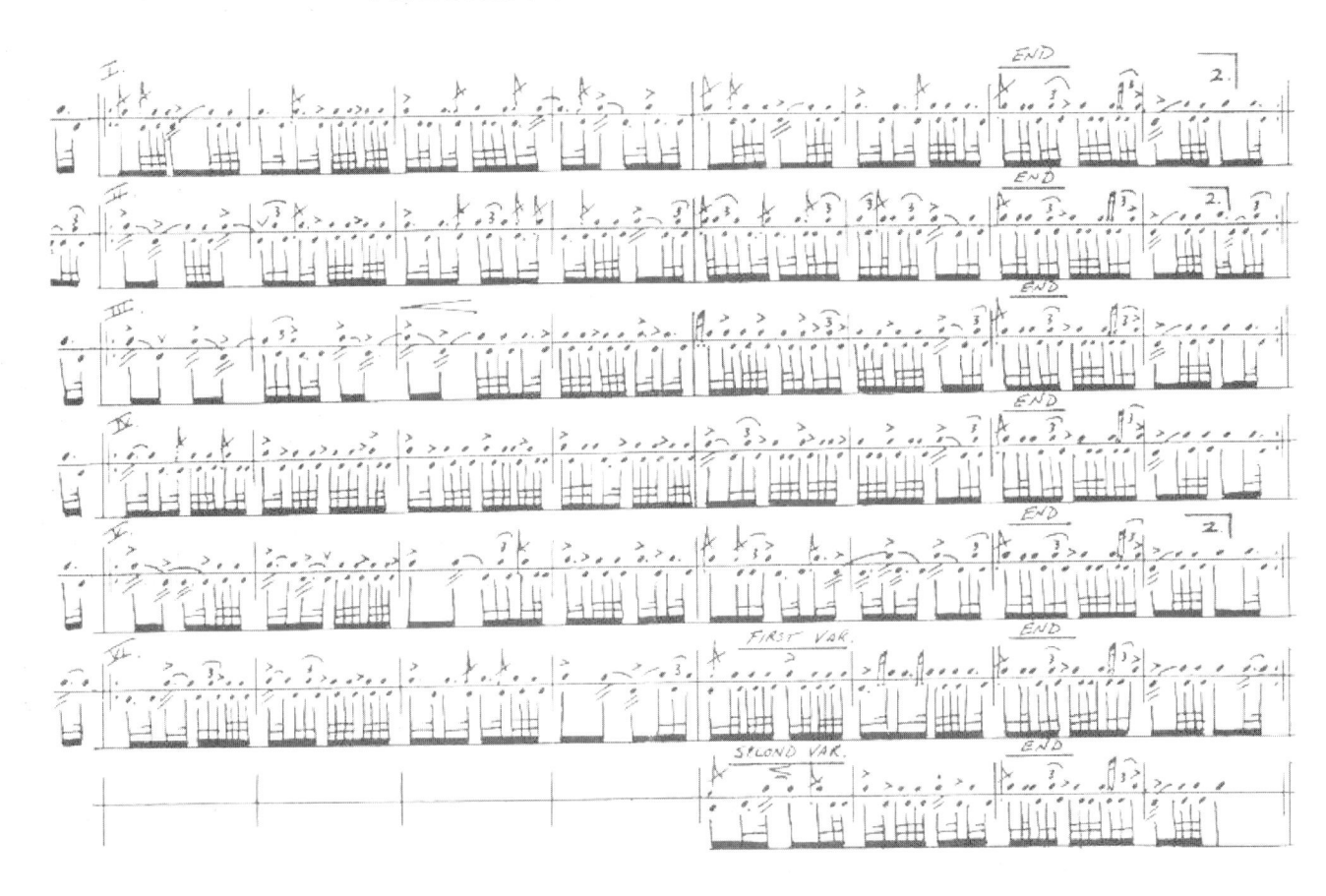

HIGHLAND WEDDING

Gordon Parkes

The Highland Wedding

2/4 March Gordon Parkes 1993

DRUM MAJOR JOHN SCULLION
SHOTTS & DYKEHEAD CALEDONIA PIPE BAND
SCOTTISH POWER PIPE BAND

John Scullion was born in Ballaghy, Northern Ireland, where he was first taught drumming by his father in the early 1960's. An astute pupil, he was soon playing his local pipe band's competition scores.

Keen to further his progress, John decided to move to Scotland to learn under the legendary Drum Major Alex Duthart. He joined the Shotts corps where he played from the 1970's until the mid 1980's, and then succeeded Alex as L/D when Alex left Shotts to join the British Caledonian Airways Band.

In 1984, the Shotts drum corps, led by John, won the Worlds Drumming Championships. A few years later he was given the opportunity to take over the drum corps of the Scottish Power Pipe Band. He accepted the challenge, both because of his great love of serious competition activity and of the number of talented drummers already in the drum corps.

The Scottish Power band enabled John the opportunity to gain many further successes on the contest field as well as the chance to travel and perform in other countries like the USA, China, Japan, Italy, Mexico and Turkistan.

On the solo circuit, John has won the RSPBA World Solo Drumming Championship four times. He has been the winner of the Glasgow and West Of Scotland Branch Solo Drumming Championships six times and on one occasion he was RSPBA Champion of Champions.

At the present time, John still leads the corps of the Scottish Power Pipe Band.

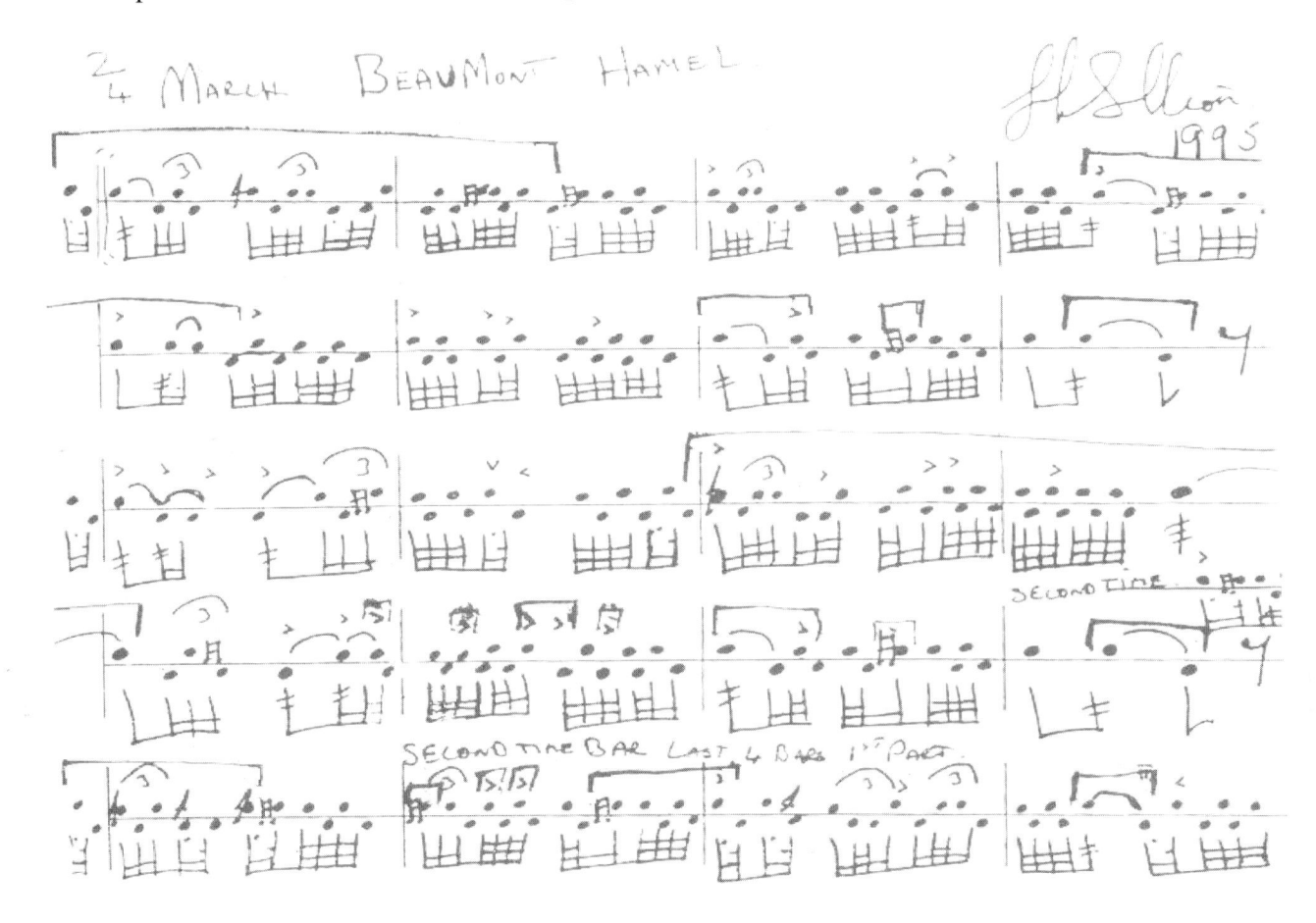

Beaumont Hamel

March   John Scullion 1995

DRUM MAJOR PAUL TURNER
ROYAL ULSTER CONSTABULARY
MCNAUGHTONS VALE OF ATHOLL
VICTORIA POLICE PIPE BAND (AUS.)
DYSART & DUNDONALD

Born in Belfast, Northern Ireland, Paul started drumming at the age of five under the tutorship of his father.

In 1977 he joined the Royal Ulster Constabulary Pipe Band and served under Billy Dunlop and then Bobby Rea.

Paul's career as a Grade One Leading Drummer started in 1984 when he held this position with the RUC. Later, this was followed by spells with the Vale of Atholl in Scotland and then with the Victoria Police in Australia.

Success has been the order of the day with his drum corps, with major titles having been won with the RUC and the Vale of Atholl, and also including World Championship second and third places with the Victoria Police.

In 1989, Paul won the World Solo Drumming Championship.

Following a short period as L/D with the Grampian Police Pipe Band, Paul is currently Leading Drummer with the Dysart and Dundonald band.

John McMillan of Barra

March Paul Turner 1990

DRUM MAJOR ERIC WARD
BRITISH CALEDONIAN AIRWAYS PIPE BAND
STRATHCLYDE POLICE PIPE BAND

Eric Ward was born in Banbridge, Northern Ireland. He started to learn pipe band drumming at the age of nine and was greatly influenced by Frank Gibson and Bobby Rea.

It was in 1979 that he moved to Scotland to join the Shotts & Dykehead Caledonia Pipe Band under the tuition of D/M Alex Duthart. When Alex left Shotts to take over the Corps of the British Caledonian Airways Pipe Band in 1982, Eric followed.

When Alex sadly passed away in 1986, Eric took over the British Caledonian corps as Leading Drummer, and under his leadership the Drum Corps won all major RSPBA Pipe Band Drum Corps Championship titles with the exception of the Worlds. Later, Eric held the position of Leading Drummer with the Polkemmet Pipe Band.

Eric Ward has also had a very successful Solo drumming career. He has won the Glasgow & West of Scotland Championships and has also been 'placed' on many occasions in that competition. In the RSPBA World Open Solo Drumming Competition, Eric has won several prizes, including Open 'Runner-up' on three occasions, the latest being in 1996.

Currently Eric is Leading Drummer of the Strathclyde Police Pipe Band and is a member of the RSPBA Adjudication Panel.

The Balmoral Highlanders

2/4 March   Eric Ward 1981

N.B.
In this score, all drags with upward stems are played closed.
Drags with downward stems are played open.(WY)

Section 9

Ancillary Information

	Page
A brief history of the Military Drum	**100**
World Pipe Band Champions	**104**
World Drum Corps Champions	**105**
World Solo Drum Champions	**106**
Index of names	**108**

A BRIEF HISTORY OF
THE MILITARY DRUM
Leading to the evolution of
PIPE BAND DRUMMING

Foreword: Although many articles have already been written on the subject of the Military Drum, "grey areas" still exist in its evolutionary history from the time of its introduction into the Western World to its acceptance and use within pipe bands. This article is an attempt to bring together disparate information from numerous sources and whilst it cannot be guaranteed that each and every item contained is strictly factual, it is a fair summary of the available wisdom to date. It should serve as broad background information to younger (and perhaps older) drummers.

One could only guess at the first drum sound created. Was it a prehistoric man accidentally striking a hollow log with a stone or a stick? Having heard it once, did he strike it again and again, enjoying its resonant sound? No one really knows. Archeological evidence from excavations and peat bog deposits indicate that drums of one kind or another have existed for around 30,000 years. There are written records of percussion instruments having existed in China circa 3000BC and there are traces to be found in India, from about the same era. There is also a poem from China, written in 1135 BC referring to "Lizard Skin Drums." From the American continent, too, evidence exists of drums being used by the Mayan and other early civilisations. The Greek and Roman armies also had their drums of one sort or another.

But it was quite a bit later than this, introduced via the Middle East or Asia Minor, that the first prototypes or precursors of the marching or military drum as we know them today, were brought to Europe by soldiers returning from The Crusades or 'Holy Wars'. These drums were often just lifted from the battlefield after fighting the Saracens and were looked upon as trophies or keepsakes. We know that the Wars of the Crusades commenced in 1096 and that the last was in 1291, so these drums first appeared in Europe somewhere around 1100 AD.

We can identify three main classes, types or sizes of drums used by the Saracens. There was the Nakareh, a very large kettledrum usually carried on the back of a camel, a smaller kettledrum called a Naqqara (later the word was corrupted to Naker), and from Persia, another even smaller drum, sometimes played with only one stick, called a Tabor (still referred to as a Tabor, Tabour, Taimbour and with versions known as Tambourin or Tambourine)

The military drum as we know it today developed from a mixture of the Tabor and the Naker. It is debatable whether it is a large Tabor or a smaller version of the Naker, but these were the first military drums with a proper shell fitted with top and bottom animal skins tensioned by ropes or thongs, to be introduced into Europe in the early 12th Century. The next time you hear a drummer referring to his instrument as "nackered", perhaps he is referring to its original name rather than it's state of play.

It would appear that the main purpose of the drum in those early days was to strike fear into the hearts of the enemy whilst strengthening the resolve of fellow soldiers. For as long as the drums continued to sound, the Colours or flags/banners were still safe. At a later stage, various predetermined drum beatings became a means of loudly confirming the order of the Commanding Officer whose vocal orders tended to be drowned in the melee and clamour of battle

In Europe, the Swiss were among the first to use drums in their armies on a regular, rather than random, basis. In fact, in the chronicles of the city of Basle, established in 1332, there is reference to drums and fifes - not fifes and drums. In England in 1492, drums were sometimes referred to as Sweche drums, recognising the Swiss as leaders in this development. Other words used were "droum" or "droume." It may be that the latter word still lingers with us, because in the British Army today, and in many other areas, the Drum Major is often referred to as the "Drummie".

Some years earlier, in 1457, the King of Hungary had large drums -Nakareh or kettledrums (so called because of their cauldron-like shape) -which were mounted on horses. These drum-horses acted as escorts when his envoys were sent to ask the French King for his daughter's hand in marriage.

In simple chronological order, some dates from military history are highlighted where this important instrument - the drum - is recorded

1527 "Scots March" composed by James V to commemorate the siege of Tantallon Castle.

1539 Parade at Westminster of "Droumes and Fyffes."

By the 16th Century, all references to Nakers, Tabors, Sweche, Droume and such had finally disappeared; the word "Drum" had firmly been established

1542 Henry VIII began to use large kettledrums (like Timpani); they came into general use in the English Army in about 1660. Later on, special carts, like a gun carriage, were used to carry the kettledrums **and** the drummers.

1545 Henry VIII's famous ship, the Mary Rose (which sank shortly after launch) carried drums; they were rediscovered when the ship was raised in 1982.

1588 Sir Francis Drake, (who earlier had fought the Spanish Armada) when on his deathbed, was supposed to have asked that his drum be carried to Plymouth to be struck in times of danger, where-upon he would return from the dead to help. Drake's drum is probably the most famous of all drums because it was perpetuated in verse by Sir Henry Newbolt.

"Take my drum to England
Hang it by the shore
Strike it when your powder's running low
If the Dons sight Devon, I'll quit the port o' Heaven
And drum them up the Channel as we drummed them long ago"

1598 There were Field or Camp Calls, known as "Reveille", played at daybreak to rouse the soldiers.

1610 A special march was first played in Prince Harry's presence. This was revived in 1632 by Charles I. It is the first written drum march. It was not broken into bars, but had sounds written to indicate each note; pou-tou, Rpoung, etc. (the early version of drummers' mouth music perhaps?) The forerunner of "Plup tup perickity plup, petup perickity plup"?

1634 First Military Discipline Manual was written with reference to "Drums and Drum Majors." The army drummer was comparatively well paid because he had various important duties to perform. In addition to playing the correct beatings for the various commands, he often had to be proficient in different languages in order to act as Interpreter, carrying messages to and from the enemy. He also often dealt out the punishment by flogging, as ordered by senior personnel. He had to do it well too or risk finding himself on the receiving end. He also was on duty at funerals.

1720 The Sultan of Turkey presented an entire military band to the King of Poland, incorporating percussion instruments never before seen or heard in Europe.

The ensemble comprised of bass drum, deep (but portable) kettledrum, tambourine, cymbals, triangle, and what was referred to as a "Jingling Johnnie". This was like a shortened version of a drum major's staff, but with a Turkish Crescent fixed at right angles across it. From the crescent dangled little bells and coloured plumes and ribbons. At the top of the staff was a small conical or umbrella-shaped cap from which other bells were suspended. The type of music played by this group was referred to as "Janissary Music".

The musicians, of course, coming from Turkey were dark-skinned men, and this whole colourful presentation was the envy of all and sundry. It became the "in-thing" to have black men as drummers wearing very colourful costumes. It has been suggested that the wearing of leopard skins by bass drummers relate to the introduction of black men into such bands. However, a separate school of thought claims that British Army officers who went big game hunting while serving in India and Africa encouraged the habit. It was a means of putting the animal skins to good use, and these sometimes carried a silver plate inscribed with the officer's name and regiment.

1746 In the Regiment of the Foot Guards, there is a reference to pipes, oboes, trumpet and side drum or snare drum. No mention of fifes here - they were obviously falling out of favour about this time.

1762 The Royal Artillery Band was formed.

1810 Samuel Potter wrote the first drum manual using staff notation as we know it. The manual was called "The Art of Beating a Drum" and written on the 'C' space of the 'F' clef.

1812 He also produced "Potters Drum, Flute and Bugle Duty Tutor," which, as a manual of drum instruction was accepted in 1817 as the universal standard to be used by the military.

Samuel Potter was a cousin of Richard Potter, a well-known flute maker. His son, William Henry Potter also made flutes and drums. The various family names concerning the famous Potter musical businesses tend to be a bit confusing. Although Samuel Potter wrote the first manual and started selling drums and other musical instruments, he registered the business in his infant son's name "Henry Potter and Co". This was because he (Samuel) was a regular soldier and could not do business with his employer (the Army). There were two Potter's music businesses when Samuel died. His other son, George, had started out on his own too.

Incidentally, the bass drums at that time (around 1810-1815) were very wide, about twice the diameter of the skin or head. The drum was slung from the waist, not the shoulders.

It was 1834 before the first use of a tenor drum is recorded. It was used in the band of The Royal Artillery. It is worth noting that this reference to tenor drum actually means tenor drum, as we know it today, (with a relationship to bass and snare drum sounds). Drums, which looked something like today's tenor drums, were in use long before 1834 but were played in the manner of a solo snare or side drum with hard or soft sticks.

1833 The formation of the first purely civilian brass band. It was a Works Band called "Walkers and Hardmans" and boasted 24 players.

1853 Only 20 years later the number of brass bands had increased to the extent that the first National Brass Band Contest was held at Belle Vue in Manchester, England

So much for the drum on its own and for military and brass bands. What about pipers and pipe bands? We have to go back a little way to examine the genealogy of this. Back in fact to 1794.

1794 This was the year in which the British army regiment, The Gordon Highlanders, was raised. It should be noted that, on the 'official roll' or registration of all ranks, no pipers are mentioned, but drummers with a rank and a relevant pay structure were included.

1796 Pipers are mentioned in "Routine Orders". Even this first reference sounds a bit demeaning. The instruction was that pipers had to attend all fatigue duties, presumably to try to lighten the burden of the soldiers doing the chores. One angry piper, when told that he could not be officially included on the records of the regiment as a piper, is said to have voiced his opinion about the huge injustice of drummers being registered. "They who only battered on dried sheep skins, requiring little skill, while he a piper - was a musician".

Some things never change.

1805 On the 11th day of May, a piper, Alexander Cameron, was taken onto the official strength of the regiment; however, he was recorded as a drummer. There was still no official category for a piper. It is interesting to note that the correct and accurate description of the Gordon Highlanders Pipe Band is "Drums and Pipes of the Gordon Highlanders", not Pipes or Pipers and Drummers of the Gordon Highlanders.

1848 The 1st Pipe Band? There is an unsubstantiated story relating to The 79th Highlanders on board a fog-bound ship en route to Quebec. Pipers and drummers were apparently ordered to play on deck in order to warn other shipping of their presence.

1854 A few chosen Scottish regiments were given permission to have "5 pipers and a Pipe Major." Although these were the first official groups of bagpipers, we know from records that unofficial ones had already existed from long before this date.

With the formal establishment of regimental pipers, the formation of pipe bands probably commenced - the first claimed by some to be The Gordon Highlanders. There is of course, some uncertainty as to the actual first band - official or unofficial. It was 1881 before all Highland Regiments received permission to formally include pipers on their roll calls but the general consensus is that one of the Scottish Regiments had the first formally recognised pipe band, probably around 1854/55.

It is difficult to establish when purely civilian bands were actually formed although records of Militia/Civilian bands exist. For instance, The City of Edinburgh Rifle Volunteers were formed in 1859, maintaining a pipe band and a brass band from the outset. Generally speaking, when pipers and drummers had completed their service in the army, it would have been around this time that civilian pipe bands would have begun to form. Many enthusiastic groups existed and inevitably began competing with each other. Individuals emigrated to other countries within the British Empire, as it was then, and continued to cultivate their music in their new surroundings. Piping and Pipe Band Associations were formed as early as the 1920's in Canada, Australia and New Zealand.

The skills of pipe band drummers have increased dramatically since these early days and this publication illustrates the gradual technical progress developed by some of the individuals involved in the evolution of Pipe Band Drumming over the past 100 years or so.

Bibliography References:
Percussion Instruments and their History by James Blades; **Military Music** by Henry George Farmer; **Handel's Kettledrums and other papers on military music** by Henry George Farmer, Ph.D., D.Litt., Hon Mus.Doc.; **The Drum** by Hugh Barty-King; The Mitchell Library, Glasgow.

World Pipe Band Champions

YEAR	BAND	PIPE MAJOR
1906	1st Highland Light Infantry	J.MacDougall Gillies
1907	3rd Lowland Volunteer Regt.	Edwin I. Macpherson
1908	5th Highland Light Infantry	J.MacDougall Gillies
1909	Stonehouse Pipe Band	Hector MacInnes
1910 -12	5th Highland Light Infantry	J.MacDougall Gillies
1913	7th Highland Light Infantry	Farquhar MacRae
1914 - 18	World War 1 - No Contests	
1919	Edinburgh City Police	Hugh Calder
1920	City of Glasgow Police	William Gray
1921 - 23	The Clan MacRae Society	William Fergusson
1924	Millhall Pipe Band	George D. MacDonald
1925	The Clan MacRae Society	William Fergusson
1926	Millhall Pipe Band	George D. MacDonald
1927 - 28	MacLean Pipe Band	William Sloan BEM
1929	Glasgow Corp. Tramways	Gavin L.Robertson
1930	Millhall Pipe Band	George D. MacDonald
1931	Glasgow Corp. Tramways	Peter Fleming
1932 - 34	The Clan MacRae Society	John F. Nicoll
1935	MacLean Pipe Band	William Sloan BEM
1936 - 39	City of Glasgow Police	John MacDonald
1940 - 45	World War 2 - No Contests	
1946	City of Glasgow Police	John MacDonald
1947	Bowhill Colliery (1st SPBA Champs.)	C.Sutherland
1948	Shotts and Dykehead Cal.	T.McAllister Snr BEM
1949	City of Glasgow Police	J.MacDonald
1950	Edinburgh City Police	D.S.Ramsay BEM
1951	City of Glasgow Police	J.MacDonald
1952	Shotts and Dykehead Cal.	T.McAllister Snr.BEM
1953	The Clan MacRae Society	A.MacLeod
1954	Edinburgh City Police	D.S.Ramsay BEM
1955 - 56	Muirhead and Sons	J.Smith
1957 - 60	Shotts and Dykehead Cal.	J.K.McAllister
1961	Muirhead and Sons	J.Smith
1962	277(A&SH) Regt. (TA)	J.Weatherston MBE BEM
1963 - 64	Edinburgh City Police	I.McLeod
1965 - 69	Muirhead and Sons	R.Hardie
1970	Shotts and Dykehead Cal.	J.K.McAllister
1971 - 72	Edinburgh City Police	I.McLeod
1973 - 74	Shotts and Dykehead Cal.	T.McAllister Jnr.
1975	Edinburgh City Police	I.McLeod
1976	Strathclyde Police	I.McLellan BEM
1977 - 78	Dysart and Dundonald	R.Shepherd
1979	Strathclyde Police	I.McLellan BEM
1980	Shotts and Dykehead Cal.	T.McAllister Jnr.
1981 - 86	Strathclyde Police	I.McLellan BEM
1987	78th Fraser Highlanders (Canada)	W.Livingstone
1988 - 91	Strathclyde Police	I.McLellan BEM
1992 - 93	Field Marshall Montgomery	R.Parkes
1994	Shotts and Dykehead Cal.	R.Mathieson
1995 - 96	Simon Fraser Univ. (Canada)	T.Lee
1997	Shotts and Dykehead Cal.	R.Mathieson
1998	Victoria Police (Australia)	N.Russell
1999	Simon Fraser Univ. (Canada)	T.Lee
2000		

N.B. Prior to 1947 -- all World Championships were held at Cowal, Dunoon

World Drum Corps Champions

YEAR	BAND	DRUM MAJOR
1947	The Clan MacRae Society	J. Cairns
1948	Renfrew	A. MacGregor
1949	The Clan MacRae Society	W. Paterson
1950	The Clan MacRae Society	W. Paterson
1951	City of Glasgow Police	A. McCormick
1952	City of Glasgow Police	A. McCormick
1953	Dalzell Highland	A. Duthart
1954	Red Hackle Pipes and Drums	A. Ross
1955	Red Hackle Pipes and Drums	A. Ross
1956	Fintan Lalor (Eire)	C. Merrigan
1957	Shotts and Dykehead Cal.	A. Duthart
1958	Shotts and Dykehead Cal.	A. Duthart
1959	Shotts and Dykehead Cal.	A. Duthart
1960	Shotts and Dykehead Cal.	A. Duthart
1961	Shotts & Dykehead/Muirhead (tie)	A. Duthart / J. Hutton
1962	Shotts and Dykehead Cal.	A. Duthart
1963	Shotts and Dykehead Cal.	A. Duthart
1964	City of Edinburgh Police	R. Montgomery
1965	Renfrew	A. Hosie
1966	Invergordon Distillers	A. Duthart
1967	Invergordon Distillers	A. Duthart
1968	City of Edinburgh Police	R. Montgomery
1969	Shotts and Dykehead Cal.	W. Stevenson
1970	Shotts and Dykehead Cal.	A. Duthart
1971	Shotts and Dykehead Cal.	A. Duthart
1972	Strathclyde Police	A. Connell
1973	Shotts and Dykehead Cal.	A. Duthart
1974	British Caledonian Airways	J. Noble
1975	Dysart and Dundonald	J. King
1976	Dysart and Dundonald	J. King
1977	Dysart and Dundonald	J. King
1978	Shotts and Dykehead Cal.	A. Duthart
1979	Triumph Street (Can.)	W. McErlean
1980	Dysart and Dundonald	J. King
1981	Boghall and Bathgate	T. Brown
1982	Boghall and Bathgate	T. Brown
1983	Boghall and Bathgate	T. Brown
1984	Shotts and Dykehead Cal.	J. Scullion
1985	Polkemmet Grorud	J. Kilpatrick
1986	Boghall and Bathgate	T. Brown
1987	78th Fraser Higlanders (Can.)	J.R. Maxwell
1988	Shotts and Dykehead Cal.	J. Kilpatrick
1989	Shotts and Dykehead Cal.	J. Kilpatrick
1990	Shotts and Dykehead Cal.	J. Kilpatrick
1991	Shotts and Dykehead Cal.	J. Kilpatrick
1992	Shotts and Dykehead Cal.	J. Kilpatrick
1993	Shotts and Dykehead Cal.	J. Kilpatrick
1994	Shotts and Dykehead Cal.	J. Kilpatrick
1995	Shotts and Dykehead Cal.	J. Kilpatrick
1996	Shotts and Dykehead Cal.	J. Kilpatrick
1997	Shotts and Dykehead Cal.	J. Kilpatrick
1998	Shotts and Dykehead Cal.	J. Kilpatrick
1999	Simon Fraser University (Can.)	J.R. Maxwell
2000		

N.B. Prior to 1947, very few details are available.

WORLD SOLO DRUM CHAMPIONS

It is believed that Solo Drumming competitions were in existence from the 1930's. However the only information that can be found relating to any winners is that of **Charlie Davis** who won "The Individual Snare Drum Championship" in 1937. (See page numbers 16/17)

Just after the end of the 2nd World War, solo competitions were organised in a more formal manner and the winners to date are listed below. The title of the competition has altered throughout the years. From 'Individual Snare' to 'SPBA Solo', to 'RSPBA Solo', to 'Worlds Solo' Drumming Championship. At the end of the day, these titles all meant the same thing --- the winners were the very best in their own era.

YEAR	NAME
1947	G. Pryde
1948	J. Catherwood
1949	A. Duthart
1950	A. Duthart
1951	A. Duthart
1952	A. McCallum
1953	A. Duthart
1954	J. Kerr
1955	J. Neil
1956	D. Splitt
1957	J. Robb
1958	A. Helie
1959	A. Clacher
1960	W. Clark
1961	A. Duthart
1962	R. Montgomery
1963	D. Armit
1964	J. Hutton
1965	R. Barr
1966	R. Rea
1967	W. Young
1968	A. Duthart
1969	R. Montgomery
1970	J. Hutton
1971	J. Hutton
1972	J. Noble
1973	J. Hutton

YEAR	NAME
1974	R. Barr
1975	J. Noble
1976	R. Barr
1977	J. Kilpatrick
1978	J. Scullion
1979	J. Scullion
1980	J. Kilpatrick
1981	J. Scullion
1982	J. Scullion
1983	J. Kilpatrick
1984	R. Rea
1985	J. Kilpatrick
1986	J. Kilpatrick
1987	A. Scullion
1988	A. Cook
1989	P. Turner
1990	J. Kilpatrick
1991	J. Kilpatrick
1992	J. Kilpatrick
1993	A. Scullion
1994	G. Brown
1995	J. Kilpatrick
1996	J. Kilpatrick
1997	A. Scullion
1998	J. Kilpatrick
1999	No contest held
2000	

INDEX OF NAMES

Surname	First Name	Page No
Armit	Dave	51,52,106
Barnham	Billy	51
Barr	Bert	51,61,106
Barrie	Jim	23
Blackley	Jimmy	23
Boag	Bill	23
Boyd	Bert	51
Brown	Tom	61,62,77,105
Brown	Gordon	77,78,106
Cairns	Jimmy	23,105
Catherwood	Jimmy	9,15,23,24,106
Chatto	Allan	51,61,64
Clacher	Adam	39,106
Clark	Willie	51,106
Collins	Jim	77
Colville	Alex	39
Connell	Alex	39,51,61,66,105
Cook	Arthur	61,77,80,106
Corkin	Gary	77
Corr	Willie	23
Craig	Allan	77
Craig	Gordon	77
Craig	Willie	15
Cranston	Neil	77
Crawford	Geordie	23
Dalrymple	Jim	15
Darroch	Andy	15
Davis	Charlie	15,16,106
Dawson	Harvey	77
Docherty	Alex	39,51
Donovan	Paddy	15,18
Duthart	Alex	23,39,40,51,61,68,77,105,106
Faulds	Danny	9,15
Ferguson	John	23
Gibson	Frank	51
Gilchrist	Teddy	23
Gillespie	Harold	77,82
Gray	Jimmy	23,39,42
Hamilton	Alex(AD)	9,10,15
Helie	Alex	39,106
Hetherington	Bob	39
Hobbs	Wayne	61,70,
Hosie	Andy	51,105
Houlden	Jackie	77
Hunter	George	39
Hunter	Michael	77
Hutton	Jim	39,51,54,61,105,106

Surname	First Name	Page No
Jelly	Gordon	23,26
Keogh	Sean(Bisto)	23
Kerr	Jock	39,44,106
Kerr	Willie	77
Kilpatrick	Jim	61,77,84,105,106
King	James	61,72,77,105
Kirkwood	John	39,46
Kirkwood	John(Jnr)	77,86
Lawrie	Doug	61
Mac Innes	John	61
MacGregor	Alec	23,28,105
Mackay	Tom	51
Marr	Jimmy	39
Maxwell	Reid	77,89,105
McCormick	Alex	23,30,39,105
McErlean	Willie	61,105
McGregor	Alex	15
Merrigan	Tommy	15,105
Millar	David	39
Montgomery	Bob	51,56,61,105,106
Noble	Joe	51,61,74,77,105,106
Parkes	Gordon	77,90
Paterson	Willie	23,32,39,105
Pryde	Geordie	23,34,39,106
Rea	John	39
Rea	Bobby	51,61,77,106
Reynolds	Kit	39,48,51
Robb	Andy	39,106
Ross	Alex	39,105
Ross	Frank	23
Rowe	Adrian	23
Scott	Charlie	15
Scullion	Andy	77,106
Scullion	John	61,77,92,105,106
Seton	Jack	23,36
Seton	John	1,6,9,12
Splitt	Davie	39,106
Stevenson	Billy	39,51,105
Taylor	Jimmy	15
Turner	Robert	51,61
Turrant	Dan	15,21
Walls	George	77
Ward	Eric	77,96
Weir	Tom	23
Wilson	Barry	77
Young	Wilson	51,58,61,106